1=00

A449

National Anthems

Dennis McIntyre was born in Detroit and died in 1990. He was educated at the University of Michigan and Carnegie-Mellon University. His play *Modigliani* was produced Off-Broadway at the Astor Place Theatre in 1980 and in London in 1987. His next play, *Split Second*, was produced at New York's Theatre Four in 1984, with later productions in Los Angeles, London, Chicago, Detroit, Minneapolis, Atlanta and Philadelphia. *National Anthems* was originally produced at the GeVa Theatre, then further developed at the Long Wharf Theatre as a workshop and was presented there on the Main Stage in 1989. *Established Price* was produced at the Philadelphia Festival Theatre and as a workshop at the Long Wharf Theatre in 1990. He received the Avery and Jule Hopwood Award in Playwriting and Fiction, an MCA Fellowship in Playwriting, two Shubert Fellowships in Playwriting, a Rockefeller Grant for Production, the Playbill Award for Playwriting, a National Endowment for the Arts in Production and the Kennedy Center/ American Express Award in Playwriting. He taught a playwriting seminar/workshop at the University of Michigan for three years, and completed a novel, *The Divine Child*. His film work included an original screenplay for Sidney Poitier and Columbia Pictures entitled *Noble*, the screenplay of his play *Split Second* for Motown Productions, an original screenplay based on the life of Curtis Sliwa, founder of the Guardian Angels subway patrols in New York City, for director John G. Avildsen, and a film for Orion Pictures, *State of Grace*, starring Sean Penn and Gary Oldman.

DENNIS McINTYRE

National Anthems

faber and faber

First published in 2005
by Faber and Faber Limited
3 Queen Square, London WC1N 3AU

Typeset by Country Setting, Kingsdown, Kent CT14 8ES
Printed in England by Mackays of Chatham plc, Chatham, Kent

A CIP record for this book
is available from the British Library

0-571-22756-2

2 4 6 8 10 9 7 5 3 1

National Anthems was originally presented by the GeVa Theatre in Rochester, New York. The play was subsequently presented by the Long Wharf Theatre, New Haven, Connecticut, on 22 November 1988. The cast was as follows:

Leslie Reed Mary McDonnell
Arthur Reed Tom Berenger
Ben Cook Kevin Spacey

Directed by Arvin Brown
Setting by Michael Yeargan
Costumes by David Murin
Lighting by Ronald Wallace

The British premiere was presented at The Old Vic, London, on 1 February 2005. The cast was as follows:

Leslie Reed Mary Stuart Masterson
Arthur Reed Steven Weber
Ben Cook Kevin Spacey

Directed by David Grindley
Designed by Jonathan Fensom
Lighting by Jason Taylor
Sound by Gregory Clarke

Characters

Arthur Reed

Leslie Reed

Ben Cook

Setting

The Reed living room in Birmingham, Michigan,
a suburb of Detroit.

Time

Saturday 8 October 1988. Night.

Design Note

The Reed living room should be beautifully furnished.
However, its beauty should be in its subtlety.
Nothing should be on display. It also should
appear comfortable and inviting.

NATIONAL ANTHEMS

Act One

Darkness. Loud rock music. Bob Seger and the Silver Bullet Band.

Lights. Arthur and Leslie Reed's living room. Its appearance – the end of a party – quite tasteful but very conservative.

Arthur, wearing an expensive, conservative suit, sits on the couch. He plays a game on his electronic watch (the game-watch). He becomes more and more excited as he increases the game's score.

Leslie, dressed for the party, enters from the kitchen with a tray. She wears an apron over her dress. She also wears a Walkman portable tape-player, oblivious to the rock music on the stereo. She moves to him, bends down, and kisses him. He kisses her without taking his eyes off the game-watch. She begins collecting dishes, glasses, etc., and places them on the tray. She exits into the kitchen with the tray.

Arthur (*losing the game*) Shit!

He picks up a brandy snifter and sips from it. He resets the game on the game-watch and starts playing another game. The doorbell rings several times. He glances towards the front door and continues playing the game.

Ben Cook, dressed in a suit and tie and a light raincoat, can be seen through the glass in the front door. Ben rings the doorbell again, waves, and then begins pounding on the door. Leslie re-enters from the kitchen carrying the tray. She doesn't hear the pounding on the door, nor does she see Ben. She collects plates, glasses, etc., and places them on the tray. She exits into the kitchen with the tray. Ben rings the doorbell again. Arthur glances at the front door, spots Ben, stands up slowly, still continuing to play the game, and moves to the front door. He turns on the porch light and opens the door. Ben enters.

Ben (*shouting above the music*) Hi, there! (*Ben extends his right hand to Arthur. Still shouting*) My name's Ben Cook.

Arthur (*automatically shaking Ben's hand, speaking loudly*) You're who?

Ben (*louder*) Ben Cook.

Leslie re-enters from the kitchen with the tray, still wearing the Walkman. She still doesn't notice Ben. She continues collecting more dishes, glasses, etc.

(*to Arthur, loudly*) Bet you thought I was the cops, didn't you?

Arthur (*loudly*) The cops?

Ben (*loudly*) The way I was pounding on your door, you must have thought it was the cops, right?

Arthur (*glancing at the game-watch, speaking loudly*) No, I didn't think that.

Ben (*loudly*) That's too bad. I thought I did a pretty good imitation.

Leslie, the tray full, turns to exit into the kitchen and notices Ben.

(*to Leslie, loudly*) Hi, there!

Leslie glances at Arthur, and then sets the tray down. She takes off her earphones. The rock music, its loudness, startles her. She moves to the CD deck and snaps it off.

(*to Leslie, loudly*) What are you doing? That's a great album. (*to Arthur*) What's the name of it? (*Points behind him.*) Everybody in the neighbourhood wants to know. (*to Leslie*) I'm Ben Cook.

Leslie Ben Cook?

Ben I live down the block a few houses.

Leslie You do?

Ben You didn't happen to read the *Free Press* last Wednesday, did you?

Arthur *Free Press*?

Leslie Last Wednesday?

Ben That's right.

Leslie No . . .

Ben You didn't read it either?

Arthur I don't usually read the *Free Press*.

Ben You don't?

Arthur No.

Ben That's too bad. I thought maybe you people read it. Anyway, I was just on my way to another party. Over on Quarton.

Leslie (*impressed*) Quarton?

Ben Isn't that an incredible street?

Leslie (*glances at Arthur*) Yes, it is.

Ben The way it winds around the lake . . . But then I heard all the music in here, and . . . Where'd everybody go, anyway?

Arthur Home.

Leslie (*nodding*) They went home.

Ben This early? I figured, all the music, it'd still be going strong.

Arthur I just like listening to Bob Seger, that's all.

Leslie (*nodding*) He does.

Ben Bob Seger?

Arthur He's out of Detroit.

Leslie (*nodding*) He is.

Ben (*grins*) I'm glad somebody's out of Detroit.

Arthur (*glances at the game-watch*) Right . . .

Ben I'm really embarrassed. I should have looked for cars. I don't know why I didn't look for cars. (*Looks at the music system.*) You've got some system hooked up there, pal. Real crisp.

Arthur It's Danish.

Ben Danish?

Leslie Bang and Olufsen.

Ben Bang and . . .

Arthur Olufsen. (*pointing at the speakers*) They're RL 140s. I had to wait four months.

Ben RL 140s . . . Right . . . All the way from Denmark. I'll bet they cost you a fortune, didn't they?

Arthur (*nods*) You live down the street?

Ben (*moves back to the front door, motions to Arthur*) I sure do. Have a look.

Arthur moves back to the front door reluctantly.

(*to Leslie*) You, too.

Leslie moves to the front door reluctantly.

(*Points.*) Right down there. See? Second house from the corner. It's got the hundred-year-old oak tree hanging all over it. I like old trees. They give you a sense of mortality, know what I mean? And they cut out air conditioning all of June and most of July. It's got the cement steps going up to the porch. I had to put them in. It's got the green railing. I had to put that in, too. A friend of mine, Bob Parker, missed the first two coming down and landed in the street about five years ago. He was out there an hour before we found him. It's got the red awning with the white 'C' in the middle. It's got the red Horizon in the driveway. (*Glances between them.*) You still don't see it?

Arthur No, I see it . . .

Leslie It's right next to the Wagners' house . . .

Ben That's the one. Nice people, the Wagners.

Leslie (*to Arthur*) They are.

Arthur They are?

Ben I've been next to them for nine years, and we've never had an argument. They've got to be around eighty.

Leslie I know . . .

Ben They're both alcoholics.

Leslie I didn't know . . .

Ben But they keep it in the family. They never bother the neighbourhood. Except for the time Walt parked his car in the Grangers' driveway by mistake. Bill Granger had a hell of a time getting to work the next morning. He had to back over Bud Crane's lawn. Cost Bill eight thousand dollars to redo Bud's lawn. The last time I drank with the Wagners, they put away a quart of Jack Daniels. They were starting on a second quart when I left. He used to work for Pan Am. They drive to South Carolina every winter. Regular as clockwork. Six a.m. – December second. I look after their house while they're gone.

Arthur You do?

Ben Wouldn't you?

Leslie Of course we would . . .

Arthur Right . . .

Ben Exactly. What are neighbours for?

Ben moves back into the house. Leslie follows him. Arthur slowly closes the front door, turns off the porch light, and then joins them. They stay very close to Ben, who doesn't get very far into the house.

(*moving back into the house*) Anyway, it's the smallest house on the block, if you didn't notice.

Leslie No, I noticed.

Arthur You're right, it is.

Leslie (*to Arthur*) It's a very attractive house, isn't it?

Arthur (*glances at the game-watch*) It is.

Ben The thing about Birmingham, even when you've got a small house, it's still big, isn't it?

Leslie Yes, that's true . . .

Ben It's got four bedrooms. I don't need four bedrooms, but I've still got them. I bought it seventeen years ago. Five per cent.

Arthur (*slowly*) Five per cent?

Ben I was real upset. I thought I was getting stiffed, right?

Arthur Right . . .

Ben I had to put in the deck. I had to weatherproof it. The basement needed work. I probably could have gotten a better deal in Royal Oak or Berkley, and I would have been closer to work, but when you get right down to it, Birmingham's got a lot more class, doesn't it?

Leslie Yes, it does . . .

Ben Are you sure you didn't read last Wednesday's *Free Press*?

Arthur I'm sure.

Leslie I can't remember. Why?

Ben It's not that important. Really. So, you two just moved in, right?

Arthur We just moved in . . .

Leslie August eighteenth . . .

Ben You know, I usually get acquainted right off, but see, I've been covering a lot of guys on the weekends. A little extra cash – (*Points behind him.*) – mortgage money, and this is my first Saturday night off in . . . What? Close to two and a half months. What is this, anyway? Your first big party?

Arthur Actually . . .

Ben (*cutting him off*) I know the feeling. (*to Leslie*) There's nothing like breaking in a new house, is there?

Leslie No, there isn't . . .

Ben And this is one incredible house. Real solid, this house. It must have been built in the twenties. (*Points.*) You know how much that wood costs today?

Arthur starts to answer Ben.

(*cutting him off*) You can't get that wood today, that's how much it costs. And I'll tell you something else – you've done a hell of a job decorating it. I can't remember the last time I saw a house this nice.

Leslie (*impressed*) Really?

Ben Maybe when I was a kid. When they took houses seriously. When every nail counted.

Leslie Thank you.

Arthur It's not really finished yet.

Ben You could have fooled me.

Leslie Half the furniture's still on order.

Ben You're kidding? Half of it?

Arthur (*indicating the furniture*) Most of it's coming from Italy.

Ben Italy?

Arthur Milan.

Leslie Gia Aluneti.

Ben Aluneti?

Leslie We tried to get Scarpa, but you wait for ever.

Ben Scarpa, right . . . All the way from Milan . . . You people really have taste, don't you? Italian furniture, a Danish system . . . You know, I've always thought this was the prettiest house on the street. I mean, from the outside. I'm sure glad I finally got a chance to see it from the inside. It's even prettier than the outside. And don't think I didn't notice that little Toyota sitting in your driveway. That's a nice colour, silver.

Arthur (*as Leslie glances at him*) It's a BMW. 325i.

Ben A BMW? Now we're really talking money, aren't we?

Arthur It's leased.

Leslie Arthur's not sure he wants to buy it. He's still looking at a Porsche.

Arthur 928S.

Ben Those Germans really know how to put a car together, don't they? I had a VW once, when you could still afford them. It took eight years for it to fall apart on me, and that's only because it went haywire on this patch of ice Christmas Eve, five years ago, Eleven Mile and Telegraph. But a BMW . . . Maybe even a Porsche . . . You people don't happen to have anything American around this house, do you?

Leslie The kitchen. The bathroom. They're pretty much American. Except for the clocks and the scales. And the shower curtains . . .

Ben I'm just kidding. You buy what you want. It doesn't matter if it's Italian or German. As long as you like it. Nineteen forty-five – that was a long time ago. You forgive and forget. I did my house in Early American. It looks like Thanksgiving every day. But this place . . . And a BMW right out front . . . Maybe even a Porsche . . . (*to Arthur*) You must be doing well. I mean, real well.

Leslie (*putting an arm around Arthur's waist*) He's doing fine.

Ben (*to Arthur*) You just keep on doing what you're doing, and one of these days, you might even end up in Grosse Pointe.

Arthur We looked in Grosse Pointe.

Leslie It's better out here.

Arthur I just want to be out of Detroit.

Leslie We don't even want to be close.

Ben That's what I like about Birmingham. It's far enough away, but if you need to get into the city, like the Grand Prix, like the fireworks, it's only forty-five minutes. Twenty-five without traffic. And it's real friendly out here, too. Even at night. The last people who lived here . . .

Leslie The Randalls.

Arthur Roy and Barbara.

Ben Right. Roy and Barbara. They were doing real well, too. It's too bad about the lung cancer.

Leslie Lung cancer?

Ben Couldn't take the winters any more. That's why you got the house.

Leslie (*to Arthur*) I didn't know . . .

Ben Anyway, they had this Mexican cook-out one time, about three years ago, invited the whole block. By the way, that's a nice yard you've got.

Arthur It's almost an acre and a half.

Ben That beats my yard by an acre and a half.

Leslie We're going to turn it into a Japanese garden. At least that's what I'd like to do.

Ben A Japanese garden?

Leslie I've always wanted to have a Japanese garden. Lots of imported stones.

Ben A Japanese garden. That'd be real different in Birmingham.

Arthur I'd rather have a pool. Build a deck out from the back door.

Ben I don't know . . . You get tired of decks. And everybody's got a pool in Birmingham.

Leslie That's what I say.

Ben Except me. But if I had a choice, if I had your yard, I'd stick with the Japanese garden.

Leslie (*to Arthur*) See!

Ben It's a lot more original, Arthur.

Leslie (*to Arthur*) It is. Thank you, Ben. Let me take your coat.

Ben (*taking off his raincoat*) Thanks.

Arthur When I've got the money, we'll talk about it.

Leslie (*moving to a closet near the front door and hanging Ben's coat up*) It all depends on Arthur's stocks.

Ben You're in the stock market?

Arthur Right.

Ben I've never met anybody who's been in the stock market. It must be real exciting – the stock market. I mean, just to be able to pick up the paper before you go to work, and then maybe you don't have to go to work. That'd be something, next year at this time, your stocks go through the ceiling, you're sitting out in your Japanese garden, cooking hamburgers . . . Except watch out for Sheba, that German shepherd next door. The Melbournes – have you met them?

Arthur Once.

Leslie Just two weeks ago. I'd like to get to know them a little better before we bring up the dog.

Arthur (*to Leslie*) I almost backed over her Tuesday night.

Ben Tuesday night? What time?

Arthur What time?

Ben No, it doesn't matter.

Leslie What doesn't?

Ben I was just thinking about something else . . .

Arthur What?

Ben Tuesday night, that's all . . . Sheba, she's like some kind of squirrel – keeps burying bones all over the neighbourhood. I mean, she really buries them, and then she forgets about them. I ran over one with my mower once. I think it was a lamb chop. I had to get a new mower. The guy's an orthodontist. You'd think he'd know better. But a Japanese garden, the stock market, this house, a BMW, maybe even a Porsche . . . You people never stop, do you? I'll bet your parents are real proud. Real proud. And you're not that old either.

Arthur (*smiles*) Thank you, Ben.

Leslie You're very sweet. Isn't he sweet?

Ben Don't mention it. You call it the way you see it, that's all. You get a sense, you know. Now, you I've got. Arthur, right?

Arthur (*shakes Ben's hand*) Arthur Reed.

Leslie (*shakes Ben's hand*) And I'm Leslie Reed.

Ben That's a nice name, Leslie Reed. And if you didn't catch it the first three times around, the last name's Cook. C-o-o-k. A lot of people spell it C-o-o-k-e. But C-o-o-k is the common spelling.

Arthur Right. No 'e'.

Ben How long have you two been married, anyway?

Leslie Nine and a half years.

Ben Nine and a half years?! That's some kind of record these days, isn't it? I've known people, real attractive people, just like yourselves, they start out for life, but it doesn't last a week.

Leslie What's your wife's name, Ben?

Ben My wife?

Leslie You're married, aren't you?

Ben Sure. I've been married a long time.

Arthur What about kids?

Ben Kids?

Leslie Do you have any children?

Ben Sure. That's why I got married, right? (*to Arthur*) What about you?

Arthur Us?

Ben Do you have any kids?

Leslie Not yet.

Ben Why not?

Leslie (*slightly flustered, to Arthur*) We just moved in, right . . .

Arthur Right . . .

Ben A bunch of kids running around here, that'd be terrific, wouldn't it? (*Points.*) Except for the speakers, right?

Arthur Right . . .

Ben You know, it's really great to see people in love after nine and a half years. You don't see that a lot any more.

Leslie You don't, do you?

Arthur Tell him about the Sanborns.

Leslie Chris and Melissa. Chris works for Arthur. They had to come tonight. They've been married seven months, and they're thinking about getting divorced.

Ben Seven months? (*to Arthur*) That's how long I stayed in the bedroom.

Arthur Tell him about the Baileys.

Leslie Susan and Andrew. He's an ophthalmologist.

Arthur He's got a six-month waiting list.

Ben That's impressive.

Leslie If you care about your eyes, he's worth it.

Ben Six months? You could go blind waiting for him, couldn't you?

Leslie They're separating, and it's only been two years.

Ben Two years? Is that all?

Leslie They were here tonight, too. Just show. They came in separate cars.

Ben Separate cars?

Leslie It's a sure sign.

Ben Separate cars. It is.

Leslie moves to a stack of Polaroids and begins sorting through them.

Arthur It's too bad. He just bought a Jaguar XJ-S. Red. If it goes to court, she'll get it.

Ben A Jaguar XJ-S? That's kind of fancy for Birmingham, isn't it?

Arthur Forty-eight thousand plus. I feel kind of guilty. He couldn't make up his mind, so I recommended it. But I would have gone for white.

Ben Forty-eight thousand dollars? That's a lot of money.

Arthur Not today, it's not.

Ben It's not?

Arthur Besides, it's got a V-12 engine.

Ben Well, that makes all the difference, doesn't it?

Leslie (*moving to them with the Polaroids, holding out the top one*) Here they are. (*Shows it to Ben and points.*) That's Susan Bailey, and that's her husband, Andrew.

Ben Andrew, he's a handsome guy.

Arthur Sharp, too.

Leslie Arthur's been after him to lose weight.

Arthur He's working on a coronary. (*Points at the Polaroid.*) You can't see it. He's got his coat buttoned.

Leslie He's addicted to junk food.

Ben Junk food. I know how he feels.

Leslie And he went to Harvard.

Ben Harvard? You'd think he'd know how to eat. It's too bad about their marriage.

Leslie (*sorting the Polaroids*) I don't know. They're a bright couple. I don't think Susan really wants the divorce. They might work it out. (*Shows another Polaroid to Ben, points.*) That's Gil Henschel. And that's his wife, Andrea.

Ben (*looking at the Polaroid*) He's a good-looking guy, too. (*to Arthur*) Thin.

Leslie Gil's in wonderful shape. He swims an hour a day. Non-stop.

Ben Non-stop?

Leslie (*nodding*) Non-stop.

Ben Jesus . . .

Leslie They're our closest friends. We've known them for five and a half years. They've got two daughters. Ginny and Marian. Six and four.

Ben He must be a happy guy.

Leslie I think the kids did it.

Ben They always do.

Arthur (*to Ben*) He was doing pretty well before the kids. (*looking at the Polaroid*) This is a good shot of Andrea.

Leslie (*stares at the Polaroid, to Arthur*) It is, isn't it . . . (*to Ben*) Andrea has lovely teeth, doesn't she?

Ben (*looks at the Polaroid, nods*) Great teeth . . . You don't see teeth like that a lot . . .

Leslie We met them in (*using French pronunciation*) St Martin.

Ben (*using French pronunciation*) St Martin . . . Right. That's a terrific place to meet people.

Leslie Arthur works for Gil.

Ben (*looking at the Polaroid*) He doesn't look that old.

Leslie He's not. Thirty-one.

Arthur Thirty-four.

Leslie He told me thirty-one.

Arthur Andrea told me thirty-four.

Leslie (*pause*) Then I guess it must be thirty-four.

Arthur (*points at the Polaroid*) You can't really tell, but Gil's a world-class ice-boater.

Ben (*studying the Polaroid*) No, you can't . . .

Leslie He raced in Budapest last February.

Ben He did?

Arthur He came in third, and that's all they do over there in the winter.

Ben Budapest . . . It must have been real competitive . . .

Arthur You don't think about it.

Ben You don't?

Arthur It's too dangerous.

Ben That's what I figured. Right off.

Arthur A hundred miles an hour on ice, it feels like two hundred.

Ben Two hundred miles an hour . . . I got up to ninety in my VW once – just before I hit that patch of ice. I thought I was breaking the sound barrier.

Leslie (*shakes her head*) I don't know how he does it.

Ben I don't either . . .

Arthur He's an incredible guy, that's all.

Leslie He is.

Ben (*nods*) He must be. (*Looks at the Polaroid, to Arthur.*) And you're right. That's a real good shot. Real clear. Especially his wife. You really know how to handle a camera, don't you?

Leslie (*sorting the Polaroids*) People hate posing for Arthur. It takes for ever.

Arthur I just like to get it right, that's all.

Ben You should see my shots. Most people look like somebody else.

Leslie (*handing another Polaroid to Ben and pointing*) Chris and Melissa Sanborn. We told you about them, too.

Ben They're not getting along either, right?

Leslie No. (*holding the Polaroid*) But you can't really tell. It's too dark.

Arthur It was an accident.

Ben (*holding the same Polaroid and pointing*) Who's the guy in the middle? He really looks like somebody.

Leslie That's Russell Chapin.

Arthur He's a chief engineer at Ford. Thirty-eight. He just about runs the design department.

Leslie Russell's a genius.

Ben (*looking at the Polaroid*) He looks it.

Leslie (*pointing at the Polaroid, to Ben*) And that's his wife, Betty. He could have done a lot better.

Ben (*studying the Polaroid, nods*) He sure could have. (*Wanders away.*) Thirty-eight . . . Jesus . . . I'll bet it was one hell of a party, wasn't it? All those people getting together . . . Talking . . .

Leslie It was.

Arthur Gil said it was the best party he's been to in three years.

Leslie Gil Henschel said that?

Arthur (*to Ben*) And Gil goes to parties all over the world.

Leslie (*to Arthur*) I'll have to write Gil a note.

Arthur You don't have to write him a note.

Leslie I'd like to write him a note, Arthur.

Arthur We gave the party.

Leslie I'd still like to write him a note.

Ben (*glancing between them*) I'll tell you one thing. A chief engineer at Ford Motor, an ice-boater, an ophthalmologist . . . You two really know a lot of interesting people, don't you?

Arthur We didn't plan it that way. It just happened.

Ben No, I've been around. You can't kid me. It's chemistry. That's what makes it happen.

Leslie (*to Arthur*) Did you hear that?

Arthur Ben?

Ben What?

Arthur You want to know something?

Ben What's that?

Arthur (*charmingly, but insincerely*) You seem like a pretty interesting guy yourself. Doesn't he?

Leslie (*similarly charmingly*) He does.

Ben I'm just a neighbour, that's all.

Arthur I'm glad he took the initiative, aren't you?

Leslie We're not that good at it. It might have been two years before we met you.

Ben I kind of make it a point to meet new neighbours. You never know when you might need them.

Leslie Exactly.

Arthur What would you like to drink, Ben?

Ben Look, if I'm intruding, just let me know, and I'll beat it out the door. It's been a long night. Your first big party in a new house. All your close friends. I know what that's like . . .

Arthur You're a neighbour, right?

Ben Right . . .

Arthur You made the effort to meet us, right?

Ben Right . . .

Leslie Then you're not intruding. Really.

Ben You just let me know when you're tired, and you won't even see me leave.

Arthur What would you like to drink, Ben?

Ben I don't need a drink right now.

Arthur What about a beer?

Ben I don't need a beer. Don't get me wrong. I drink beer. Everybody drinks. Unless they're dead, right? (*Pats his jacket pocket.*) I'm just carrying my own tonight, that's all. It was a gift. My wife gave it to me. Maybe I'll have a beer later.

Arthur We've got a lot of beer left.

Leslie That's right. (*to Arthur*) Nobody drank beer tonight, did they?

Arthur Just let me know when you want one.

Ben Thanks. I will. I'll bet it's German beer, right?

Arthur Danish.

Leslie (*picks up the tray, moves towards the kitchen*) If you don't mind, Ben, I'll just finish cleaning up. It won't take that long.

Ben Sure. You do whatever you want. It always looks better clean, doesn't it? Especially this place. It even looks good dirty. Don't worry. I'll keep him occupied.

Arthur Sit down, Ben.

Ben Sure. You don't have a special place or anything, do you? (*Points.*) Here?

Arthur Sit anywhere you like.

Ben (*glances around, then sits down on the couch*) Where'd you live before Birmingham?

Arthur Southfield. (*He takes a cigarette out of a cigarette box on the coffee table and quickly lights it with a table lighter on the coffee table.*)

Ben I'm probably dating myself, but I can remember when you could take a walk in Southfield and you'd trip over a pheasant. It sure has changed, Southfield, hasn't it?

Arthur (*inhaling quickly*) Yes, it has.

Ben Like I said, I'm probably dating myself.

Leslie's footsteps can be heard re-entering from the kitchen.

Arthur (*handing the cigarette to Ben*) Here.

Ben I don't smoke.

Arthur Just hold it.

Ben (*holding the cigarette awkwardly*) Sure.

Leslie re-enters carrying the tray. She is again wearing the earphones. She is listening to a Japanese language tape. She pronounces the Japanese words and phrases as she goes about collecting dishes, cleaning.

(*to Arthur*) What do you do, anyway?

Arthur (*sitting down*) I'm an attorney: Donovan, Bates, Gulliver and Henschel.

Ben Is that out here?

Arthur It's downtown. (*watching Leslie begin to exit*) The Renaissance Centre.

Ben A lawyer? That's terrific.

Leslie exits with the full tray. Arthur quickly gets up, takes the cigarette from Ben, sits back down again, and then inhales it, leaning his head back.

(*Looks around the living room and nods.*) So, that's how you did it. The law, that's great. We need all the lawyers we can get, and I think we've got them. Except for the ones in jail. But there's always room for one more isn't there?

Arthur (*slowly exhaling the smoke*) What . . .

Ben Just a little bit of humour there, that's all.

Leslie's footsteps can be heard re-entering from the kitchen. Arthur quickly gets up and hands the cigarette back to Ben. Arthur sits back down as Leslie re-enters carrying a bottle of Windex and some paper towels. She moves to the coffee table, kneels next to it, takes everything off it, sprays the glass top, wipes it dry, and then carefully sets everything back on it, all the time listening to her Walkman tape-player and pronouncing the Japanese words and phrases.

(*as Leslie re-enters*) No, the law, that's really special. I mean, everybody's going around suing everybody else these days, right? So, there's got to be somebody to set it all straight, doesn't there?

Arthur Yes . . .

Ben Do you go into court a lot?

Arthur It depends on the case. It's basically corporate. Taxes. Shelters.

Ben Shelters, right . . . What would we do without shelters?

Arthur activates the game-watch and begins to play a game on it.

Arthur Don't mind me, Ben. I've been trying to beat this sucker for two days. It's a classic. You can't get them any more.

Ben No, you go ahead . . .

Arthur I've just about got it figured out.

Ben It looks like a lot of fun . . .

Arthur nods, concentrating on the game.

Remember those Ataris?

Arthur nods, concentrating on the game.

If you didn't have an Atari, you didn't invite people over, right? Everybody I knew was putting an Atari on plastic. Two or three if they had kids. Now they're all sitting out in garages, and they're still paying them off, charging VCRs on top of them. That's the great thing about this country – you never get out of debt, but you can always invite people over.

Arthur Warner Communications.

Ben Warner Communications?

Arthur They couldn't top the 5200. That's what screwed them. They should have stuck with the 2600 and skipped the detail.

Ben People get tired of detail real fast, don't they? My mother used linen napkins all the time, even if it was just breakfast. My old man was always dirty from the mills. He liked linen napkins. You don't see that much any more, do you? (*looking at the game-watch*) What's this one called?

Leslie finishes with the coffee table and exits into the kitchen with the bottle of Windex and used paper towels.

Arthur *Firing Squad.*

Ben *Firing Squad* . . . Is it tough?

Arthur (*losing the game*) Shit! (*Glances up.*) What?

Ben (*of the game-watch*) Is it tough?

Arthur (*beginning a new game*) I just about had it.

Ben What happened?

Arthur It keeps getting random.

Ben Random?

Arthur (*of the game-watch*) It's not as bad as pinball.

Ben Pinball?

Arthur It's got five games on the chip.

Ben The chip? Right . . .

Leslie re-enters still wearing the Walkman and listening to the Japanese tape. She carries a hand-vacuum. She begins vacuuming various spots on the rug around Ben and Arthur, both of them lifting up their feet as she vacuums underneath them.

Arthur (*talking above the vacuum*) You sure you don't want a drink?

Ben (*talking above the vacuum*) No, I'm fine.

Arthur (*looking at the game-watch*) I just want to figure out if it's me or the chip.

Ben I know the feeling . . . (*looking at the game-watch*) Does it have the time, too?

Arthur I didn't buy it for the time. I've got a Rolex for the time.

Ben A Rolex? That's fantastic.

Arthur Seventy-two-hundred-dollars fantastic.

Ben Seventy-two hundred dollars?

Leslie stops vacuuming.

(*speaking too loudly*) You really know what time it is, don't you?

Leslie glances around the room, and then exits into the kitchen with the hand-vacuum.

Arthur I can't figure it out. (*Goes towards the kitchen.*) Leslie? (*louder*) Leslie?

Ben I think she's wearing earphones.

Arthur (*turning back to Ben*) What?

Ben I think she's wearing earphones.

Arthur (*moving towards the hallway leading to the kitchen*) I'll be right back. (*He stops at the edge of the hallway.*) Leslie? (*Louder.*) Leslie?

Leslie (*off*) What?

Arthur What happened to the directions?

Leslie (*off*) What directions?

Arthur The watch Gil gave me.

Leslie (*off*) They're in the game closet, aren't they?

Arthur Whereabouts in the game closet?

Leslie (*off*) Find the box. I left them in the box.

Arthur Do you want to watch Ben for a minute?

Ben Don't worry about me. I'm fine.

Leslie (*off*) I'll be right out, Ben. I just want to turn on the dishwasher.

Arthur exits. Ben stares down at the cigarette, and then fans the smoke out of his face. The barely audible sound of a dishwasher is heard until it completes its cycle. Arthur is heard rummaging through the game closet upstairs. Leslie re-enters from the kitchen carrying a 'designer' tray made out of wood. The tray contains a glass of white wine and a small plate of shrimp puffs. She sets the tray down, and then sets the glass of wine on a coaster. She takes the remains of the cigarette from Ben, careful not to drop the ash, and rubs it out in an ashtray.

Ben That's a pretty tray.

Leslie (*taking cocktail napkins from a drawer*) It's West German. (*Offers the plate of shrimp puffs.*) Shrimp puff?

Ben Sure.

Leslie hands him a cocktail napkin, setting the rest of the napkins on the table. Ben picks a shrimp puff, changes his mind, puts it back on the plate, and then picks another one.

Thank you. (*Ben has difficulty chewing the shrimp puff. It takes a few minutes before he finally swallows all of it. Beginning to chew it.*) Good.

Leslie picks up her glass of wine and sits down opposite Ben.

(*chewing harder*) Real good. (*Nods towards the upstairs.*) He's really crazy about that game, isn't he?

Leslie (*sipping her wine*) If it's a gadget, Arthur's obsessed. If it's a game, he's even worse. I can't understand it. I'm bored after two minutes. But it's good for him. All those missiles crashing into each other. It takes his mind off the world.

Ben (*looking around the living room*) You sure did a good job.

Leslie Thank you, Ben.

Ben You can't even tell there was a party.

Leslie (*pointing to the couch*) There's a wine stain behind that cushion.

Ben It's a good thing you can't see it.

Leslie But you know it's there.

Ben (*looking around the living room*) The law, it's really profitable, isn't it?

Leslie It is for Arthur. But he works hard at it. Ten, eleven hours a day.

Ben What about you? Do you work, too? Or does he just keep you busy running back and forth to the bank all day depositing cheques?

Leslie (*looking around the house*) At eleven and a half per cent?

Ben You pay eleven and a half per cent?

Leslie Arthur wanted a fixed rate. No, I work.

Ben (*glancing around the room*) Eleven and a half per cent . . . Jesus. What do you do?

Leslie I teach.

Ben What do you teach?

Leslie Music and art.

Ben Music and art. Now there's a couple of areas I completely missed. I'm really deficient when it comes to music and art. Except jazz. I've got a pretty good jazz collection. But music and art, teaching it, that's really classy. And there's a lot of music, a lot of art, so you must have an exceptional memory, right?

Leslie I have lesson plans. It's not that hard. Everything's laid out, and they won't let you change it that much.

Ben But you still had to learn it, right? How come you picked music and art?

Leslie I play the flute. I've always like to draw.

Ben The flute, that's really something. You must have great breath control.

Leslie That's part of it . . . But it's mostly practice, that's all.

Arthur re-enters, moving down the stairs, holding a set of directions, reading them as he walks. He sits down and continues to read them, occasionally fiddling with the game-watch.

Ben Whereabouts do you teach? Out around here?

Leslie Sacred Heart. Bloomfield Hills.

Ben All girls. That must be nice.

Arthur Rich girls.

Ben That's what I've heard.

Arthur One hundred thirty thousand a year, that's the median income.

Ben That much? I'll bet they get a real good education, don't they?

Leslie Seven hundred and forty on the college boards. That's the average.

Ben Seven hundred and forty . . . That must be hard to beat . . . It's got a pretty campus, Sacred Heart. I've passed it a lot. (*suddenly a bit distant*) Lots of trees . . . Maple trees. Real healthy maple trees. Lots of grass, too. There's always somebody cutting it in the summer. One of those mowers with an umbrella on it. Even when the sun's out . . . I wonder what he thinks about . . .

Arthur Sixty-three acres, that's what he thinks about.

Ben (*snapping back*) Sixty-three? I've only seen it from the street. It must really go back.

Arthur You know what it's worth? One acre?

Ben No. What?

Arthur Tell him.

Leslie Arthur, Ben's not interested in land values.

Arthur Four hundred and eighty thousand.

Leslie (*to Ben*) Five hundred and twenty-five.

Arthur Del told me it was four hundred and eighty.

Leslie Arthur, I work there.

Arthur Five hundred and twenty-five . . . Jesus . . . (*to Ben*) They bought it back in the twenties, when there wasn't anything out here. Two thousand an acre. I wish I'd been around in those days.

Ben If you'd been around in those days, you'd be dead now.

Leslie Please, let's not talk about death.

Ben It was just a joke . . .

Leslie I know, but we just lost a close friend.

Ben I'm sorry . . .

Arthur About eight or nine months ago.

Leslie It was two months ago, Arthur.

Arthur Two months? I thought it was longer. I can't believe he's still dead.

Ben No, that's hard . . .

Leslie Arthur?

Arthur What?

Leslie Do you realise what you just said?

Arthur What?

Leslie Never mind. He was hang-gliding.

Ben Hang-gliding . . . Right . . . I've always wanted to try hang-gliding . . .

Arthur He walked off a cliff in California. Right off it. Six hundred feet. Straight down.

Leslie Of course it was straight down.

Arthur I was just telling him, that's all.

Ben It must have been fast . . . Nothing holding him up . . .

Leslie There wasn't a cloud in the sky. That's what we heard.

Ben Not a cloud in the sky . . . I guess you can't blame the weather, can you? . . .

Leslie Thirty-six years old. He left a wife and three children.

Ben That's real sad.

Leslie He left them in Grosse Pointe.

Ben That's even worse . . .

Leslie (*to Arthur*) That's why I worry about Gil and his ice-boats. (*to Ben*) All he needs is one bad accident.

Ben (*agreeing*) That's all he needs. A hundred miles an hour on ice, you'd be lucky if they found your eyebrow.

Arthur (*to Leslie*) Gil's a risk taker. He's got the money to take risks. (*to Ben*) He wouldn't be happy without risks.

Ben (*agreeing*) No, he wouldn't.

Leslie (*to Arthur*) That was Carl's philosophy, too. I think he might have changed it if he could have seen what he looked like splattered all over those rocks.

Ben (*to Leslie*) He probably went into shock. (*to Arthur*) You don't feel anything if you're in shock.

Arthur (*to Leslie*) Let's not start. All right?

Leslie I still worry about him.

Arthur I'm sure he appreciates it.

Leslie (*to Ben*) I don't know what they have to prove.

Ben (*agreeing*) I don't either.

Arthur Leslie, I said, let's not start.

Leslie and Arthur stare at one another. Leslie forces a smile. Ben glances between them. Leslie turns away and sips her wine. Arthur shuts off the game-watch and tosses the instructions on the coffee table.

Arthur It's got to be the chip. It's not doing what it's supposed to be doing.

Leslie (*icily*) You couldn't find it in the directions?

Arthur (*pauses*) I read them three times. (*to Ben*) It's got to be the translation.

Leslie (*holds out the plate*) Would you like another shrimp puff?

Ben (*too loudly*) No.

Arthur nods, picks up his brandy, and sips it. Leslie sips her wine. Ben stares at the instructions, places them back on the table, and then drums his fingers on his knees.

Arthur What do you do, Ben?

Ben Me?

Arthur That's right.

Leslie What do you do for a living?

Ben Me?

Arthur You.

Ben You people wouldn't be interested in what I do . . . Not you people. I'm just a working stiff, that's all . . . So, what do you say? Let's cut out the shop talk. Monday's only a day away, and this is our night off, right? (*Glances at the instructions, then tosses them on the coffee table.*) I know . . . You people like games. What do you say to a little bit of 'The Name of the Game Is'?

Leslie (*to Arthur*) 'The Name of the Game Is'?

Arthur Beats me.

Ben Haven't you people ever played 'The Name of the Game Is'?

Arthur No.

Leslie I've never heard of it.

Arthur What exactly is it?

Ben What is it? It's the best drinking game ever invented, that's what it is.

Leslie It is?

Ben You wait.

Arthur How's it work?

Ben It's real simple. First of all, you just get a rhythm going. Like this.

Ben slaps his knees twice, claps his hands together twice, slaps his knees twice, claps his hands together twice, etc.

That's the rhythm. You keep it going. Lots of speed.

Arthur Ben?

Ben What?

Arthur Is this generally considered an adult game?

Ben I know guys, twenty years older than me, they get a few sheets to the wind, and right off, bang, 'The Name of the Game Is' comes out of the bag. Don't get me wrong. It's not like chess, but it still takes a lot of concentration. It's a Saturday-night game. Like now. It livens things up, that's all. (*suddenly a bit distant*) It's for celebrating . . . That's what it's for . . .

Leslie Ben?

Ben (*snapping back*) Let's get the rhythm down, and then I'll explain the rest of it.

Ben begins the rhythm again. Leslie, being polite, begins the rhythm. Arthur slowly begins the rhythm, his clapping very unenthusiastic and out of sync with Ben and Leslie's clapping.

Now, if I'm first man up, top of the order, on the clap, I name a category. You know, like cars, movie stars, presidents, countries, streets in Birmingham, and then, when it's your turn, starting clockwise, you have to name something in that category. If you can't name something on the first clap, then you lose. And you can't repeat either. That's one of the rules. If I name something, and you repeat it, that's the end of the game. Loser drinks, and then he starts the next game. It's basically a beer game. Chug a bottle. Go through a case.

Arthur and Leslie stop clapping. Ben stops too.

Arthur Ben?

Ben What?

Arthur Do you mind if I ask you something?

Ben Feel free.

Arthur What's the point of this game?

Ben The point of the game is, the more you lose, the more you drink. And the more you drink, the more you lose.

Leslie I see . . .

Arthur It sounds fascinating, Ben.

Leslie It does, doesn't it?

Ben I know what you're thinking, but it's not that easy. Really. All right, let's get the rhythm going, and I'll take the first shot.

Ben enthusiastically begins the rhythm again. Leslie begins the rhythm again, with less enthusiasm than Ben. Arthur begins the rhythm again, with the same lack of enthusiasm as before.

Faster. Harder. The rhythm, that's what makes it tricky. You've got to concentrate on two things at once.

Arthur (*to Leslie*) Lots of rhythm in this game.

Leslie (*to Arthur*) Lots of it.

Ben Everybody ready?

Arthur and Leslie nod.

Here we go! (*Claps.*) The name of – (*Claps.*) – the game is – (*Claps.*) – baseball players!

Arthur (*clapping*) Alan Trammell.

Leslie continues the rhythm, unable to come up with a name.

Ben Game's over! (*to Leslie*) You lost!

All stop the rhythm.

Leslie That wasn't a very long game, was it?

Ben (*to Leslie*) And you thought it was easy, didn't you?

Arthur How could you possibly lose? You watch the Tigers.

Leslie I watch the Tigers, but I don't know their names.

Arthur You watch a game a weekend, and you don't know their names?

Leslie I watch a game a weekend because you watch a game a weekend. (*to Ben*) I'd rather read.

Arthur If you watch a game a weekend, then you've got to know at least one name.

Leslie I know their numbers.

Arthur How can you know their numbers and not know their names?

Ben (*to Arthur*) I told you it was a tough game.

Arthur It's not a tough game! She just doesn't know shit about baseball!

Leslie (*to Ben*) I was going to say Alan Trammell. It was right on the tip of my tongue. (*to Arthur*) But you had to say it first, didn't you?

Arthur Leslie, there's more than one baseball player in the world. Do you know how many baseball players there are in the world? Do you know how many famous baseball players there are in the world? Do you have any idea? Right off, there's Kirk Gibson.

Ben (*nods*) Kirk Gibson.

Arthur You can't read a paper without spotting his name. And what about Detroit? We live in Detroit. Chet Lemon. Jack Morris. Orlando Mercado. Gary Pettis. Lou Whitaker. Larry Hendon. Tom Brookens. Dave Bergman. Luis Salazar. Mike Henneman. They're all over the place. They almost won the American League East last year. Two years ago, we went to the play-offs. Remember the play-offs? Game four. Game five. Game six. We went to eleven games last summer. You read the paper every day. You've got to see their pictures in the paper.

Leslie I'm not interested in the sports section. (*to Ben*) I automatically close the paper when I come to it. Or I skip over to the obituaries.

Ben (*nods*) The obituaries . . . Right . . .

Arthur But you sit there. All summer. Every weekend. You watch it with me. All nine innings. (*to Ben*) She doesn't even go to the bathroom. (*to Leslie*) That Orioles game. Fourteen innings. That Red Sox game. Sixteen innings.

Ben (*unable to stand it any longer*) Give her a break, Arthur. It was the first game, that's all. I shouldn't have done sports. I should have known better.

Arthur I didn't have a problem, did I?

Ben I should have made it more universal. That's what I should have done. Something like body parts. (*to Leslie*) Just take a sip, and then you start.

Arthur (*as Leslie takes a quick sip of wine*) Alan Trammell. I don't believe it. That's it?

Leslie starts the rhythm, with much more enthusiasm. Arthur starts the rhythm, with much more enthusiasm.

Leslie (*to Arthur*) I'm going to nail your ass!

Ben (*starting the rhythm*) I told you it was a lot of fun, didn't I?

Leslie (*clapping*) The name of – (*Claps.*) – the game is – (*Claps.*) – famous painters!

Ben (*clapping*) Picasso!

Arthur (*clapping*) Van Gogh!

Leslie (*clapping*) De Kooning!

Ben (*to Arthur*) De who?

Arthur (*to Ben*) Just keep it going!

Ben Pablo!

Arthur (*stops the rhythm*) Pablo?!

Leslie (*stops the rhythm*) That's not a painter!

Ben (*continuing the rhythm*) Sure it is. Pablo Picasso.

Leslie You said you couldn't repeat! Didn't he say that?

Arthur That's what you said, Ben!

Ben I didn't repeat. The first time I said Picasso. This time I said Pablo.

Arthur It's the same painter, Ben!

Leslie It is!

Ben Pablo . . . I guess that's kind of stretching it, isn't it?

Arthur Kind of stretching it?!

Leslie That's not kind of stretching it, Ben! That's breaking your own rules!

Arthur It's flat-out cheating, Ben!

Leslie It is!

Ben (*nods slowly and takes out a silver flask*) All right. You win. I lost. (*Ben uncaps the flask, sips from it, recaps it, and then puts it back in his pocket.*)

Arthur (*shaking his head*) Pablo!

Leslie (*shaking her head*) Pablo Picasso!

Arthur Jesus! It'd be nice if it went around more than once, Ben.

Ben Don't worry. It will.

Ben thinks for a moment, and then glances at the window facing the back yard. Arthur and Leslie glance towards the window.

Ready?

Arthur *and* **Leslie** Ready!

All enthusiastically begin the rhythm.

Ben (*clapping*) The name of – (*Claps.*) – the game is – (*Claps.*) – plants!

Arthur continues the rhythm, unable to come up with a name.

(*Stops the rhythm.*) That's it, fella! You're out of the ball game!

Arthur (*stops the rhythm*) Plants?! Goddamn plants?!

Ben I was just thinking about your Japanese garden, that's all.

Leslie (*stops the rhythm*) Why didn't you just say poinsettia?

Arthur I was going to say poinsettia!

Leslie (*smiles*) Then why didn't you just say it?

Arthur I was one second away from saying it!

Leslie You still didn't say it.

Ben You could have said poison ivy. That's pretty common.

Arthur That's not a plant!

Ben It's a shrub.

Arthur Since when is a shrub a plant?!

Leslie It's the same thing, Arthur.

Arthur Look, it's called a shrub tree, right?! Poison ivy, don't hand me that shit!

Leslie What are we arguing for? It's only a game, Arthur.

Arthur (*stands up*) He comes up with plants! It's like me asking him to name the Fortune five hundred! (*Picks up his brandy.*) Plants?! Goddamn plants?! (*Arthur begins to drink his brandy too fast. He begins to cough.*)

Ben (*glancing at Leslie*) Jesus . . .

Ben quickly moves to Arthur and slaps his back. Arthur lurches forward, spilling brandy on his jacket sleeve and the floor.

Arthur (*looking at his sleeve*) Shit!

Leslie (*moving to Arthur*) What happened?

Arthur (*showing the sleeve*) Look at it!

Leslie Arthur, it's just brandy.

Arthur I just bought this suit!

Ben Did I do something?

Leslie (*to Ben*) It was an accident.

Ben (*to Arthur, pointing at the sleeve*) Did I do that?

Arthur (*to Leslie*) I just paid nineteen hundred dollars for this suit!

Leslie I know what you paid!

Ben Nineteen hundred dollars?

Arthur (*holding out the sleeve*) And look at it!

Ben That's a lot of money for a suit . . .

Leslie Arthur, it's not a tragedy. Just sponge cold water on it.

Arthur exits into the kitchen. Leslie takes a wad of cocktail napkins from a drawer, moves to the spilled brandy, and begins wiping up the spill.

I don't think this game's going to work. Ben.

Ben No?

Leslie No.

Ben Arthur doesn't like to lose, does he?

Leslie No, he doesn't.

Ben I can see that. He's real competitive, isn't he? If he wasn't, then he wouldn't have all this, would he? My mistake. 'The Name of the Game Is', it was all wrong. I should have tried magic.

Leslie Magic?

Ben I'll bet you didn't know I was a magician, did you?

Leslie No, I didn't know that . . .

Ben Do you think he'd like to see a trick?

Leslie I don't think Arthur'd like to see a trick.

Ben Everybody likes magic. I've never met anybody who didn't like magic.

Leslie You've met Arthur. Arthur knows all the tricks.

Ben He does? Then that'd make it even more of a challenge, wouldn't it?

Leslie Why don't we do it later, Ben?

Ben No, we'd better do it now. I might not remember it later. I'll need a cigarette.

Ben moves to the coffee table. He takes a cigarette out of the cigarette box. Leslie, having wiped the floor, moves towards the kitchen with the used cocktail napkins. Arthur re-enters from the kitchen, his jacket sleeve wet, rubbing it with a finger.

Leslie Did it come out?

Arthur I don't know. It's still wet.

Arthur glances at Ben. Ben holds up the cigarette.

(*to Leslie*) What are we doing now?

Leslie (*slowly*) Magic.

Arthur It's like being on a cruise ship.

Leslie exits into the kitchen with the used cocktail napkins.

Ben One trick, Arthur. If you don't like it, no more tricks. (*motioning him.*) But you've got to sit down if you really want to see it. I want you close. I don't want any complaints.

Arthur Ben, I can figure out just about every trick.

Leslie (*re-entering from the kitchen*) He can. He's good.

Ben (*holding up the cigarette*) Not this one.

Arthur I don't want to embarrass you, Ben. Really.

Leslie He doesn't.

Arthur I used to do magic when I was a kid.

Leslie He did.

Arthur I used to do a lot of magic. I used to do cigarette tricks.

Leslie I've seen him do it.

Ben Ten bucks says you can't figure this trick out.

Arthur Ten bucks?

Ben Ten bucks.

Leslie You'll lose it, Ben.

Ben I doubt it.

Arthur Ten bucks?

Ben Ten bucks.

Arthur All right. Ten bucks.

Arthur moves to the coffee table and takes another cigarette out of the cigarette box just as Ben starts to light the first cigarette with the table lighter.

(*Holds the second cigarette out to Ben.*) Use this one.

Ben (*grinning*) Sure.

Ben takes the first cigarette out of his mouth and sets it in the ashtray. Arthur and Leslie sit down. Ben lights the cigarette with the table lighter, and then offers the cigarette to Arthur.

You want a puff?

Leslie Arthur's given up smoking.

Ben That's terrific, Arthur!

Arthur Just do the trick, Ben!

Ben (*holding up the cigarette*) I need verification, that's all. This is a real cigarette, right?

Arthur takes the lit cigarette from Ben.

Leslie Don't inhale it!

Arthur (*to Leslie*) I gave it up, right? Henschel paid me the five hundred bucks, didn't he?

Arthur puffs on the cigarette without inhaling it. He starts to hand the cigarette back to Ben.

It's a real cigarette.

Ben (*pointing to the cigarette*) Touch it.

Arthur Touch it?

Ben Just make sure it's lit.

Arthur It's lit!

Ben Just make sure.

Arthur starts to hand the cigarette back to Ben.

Ben (*to Leslie*) You touch it.

Leslie I believe you.

Ben No, you've got to touch it.

Arthur holds the cigarette out to Leslie. She wets a finger and touches the cigarette, jumping back slightly.

Leslie It's lit.

Ben Fine. Could I have the cigarette back now?

Arthur hands the cigarette back to Ben. Ben unbuttons his right shirtsleeve and pushes it up his arm.

Arthur You're going to put it in your mouth, aren't you?

Ben (*to Leslie*) I admire a guy who's confident, don't you?

Arthur (*to Leslie*) I knew he was going to put it in his mouth.

Leslie Maybe he won't put it in his mouth.

Arthur He's got to put it in his mouth. I've seen it done a hundred times. I did it when I was fourteen. I've seen every variation.

Ben (*holding up his right arm*) Nothing up my sleeve, right?

Arthur *and* **Leslie** Right.

Ben glances around, and then lifts up the vase of flowers on the coffee table. He takes the linen napkin, makes a fist with his left hand, and begins to stuff the linen napkin into it.

Ben (*picking up the napkin*) You don't mind if I use this, do you?

Leslie Arthur, that's Irish linen.

Ben (*stuffing the napkin into his fist*) That feels better already.

Leslie Ben, that's Irish linen.

Ben Irish linen? (*grinning*) Jesus, I hope I do it right! (*Ben slowly pushes the cigarette, burning end first, into his fist and the napkin. Smoke rises from around his fist and the napkin. Pushing the cigarette down*) A little more. A little more.

Leslie Arthur, would you please do something!

Arthur I can't! I'm concentrating!

Ben (*still pushing the cigarette down*) And a little more. (*to Leslie*) Damn, I think I can feel it!

Leslie Arthur, stop him!

The cigarette disappears into Ben's fist, smoke still rising. Ben closes his eyes in great pain. He squeeze his fist.

Ben It's not working . . . It's not working!

Leslie (*to Arthur*) You can't mend Irish linen!

Ben screams in pain. Leslie screams at the same time, Arthur starts to stand up. Ben opens his eyes, suddenly grins, and then opens his left fist. The cigarette is gone. The napkin has no burns on it. He waves the napkin, and then hands it to Leslie. Leslie quickly inspects the napkin, and then begins laughing.

That's wonderful, Ben! (*to Arthur*) Isn't that wonderful?! How'd he do it?

Ben How'd I do it, Arthur?

Arthur grabs the napkin from Leslie and inspects it.

Leslie Well?

Arthur You want to do it again?

Leslie Pay him the ten dollars, Arthur.

Ben I don't want the money. I couldn't take it. I suckered him into it.

Arthur You want to do it again or not? Sixty bucks.

Ben I can't take the smoke. Really.

Arthur Eighty bucks.

Ben You don't want to know how I did it. That's what makes it magic.

Arthur I want to know how you did it. A hundred bucks.

Leslie Arthur, it's a secret.

Arthur (*glares at her*) Fuck the secret!

Ben It's just a trick. It's just practice. (*Takes a piece of trick rope out.*) Would you like to see another trick?

Arthur No.

Leslie I wouldn't mind seeing another trick.

Arthur I really don't want to see another trick, Ben.

Arthur tosses the linen napkin on the coffee table and sits down. Ben slowly sits down on the couch. He puts away the trick rope. Leslie moves to the coffee table, kneels, and begins to straighten it. Ben glances between them and then takes out his flask. He uncaps it and takes a sip.

Ben I hope I didn't ruin your jacket.

Arthur It's fine.

Ben takes another sip from his flask, starts to set the open flask on the coffee table, can't quite reach it, and then sets it down on the rug.

Ben Did that suit really cost you nineteen hundred dollars?

Arthur nods.

Leslie (*pointing to the flask*) Ben, I think maybe . . .

Ben (*of Arthur's suit*) It's almost a perfect fit, isn't it?

Arthur stares at Ben, and then nods.

(*looking at his own suit*) I don't wear suits that often. It's got to be an occasion.

Arthur nods.

Leslie Ben?

Ben What?

Leslie Your flask. It's on the rug.

Ben My flask?

Ben leans down to look, moves his foot, and knocks over the flask. Whisky spills on the rug. Leslie half-screams and jumps up. Arthur slowly stands up.

Leslie I knew it!

Ben (*quickly picking up the flask*) I'm really sorry. I'm not doing real well tonight, am I? Your sleeve, now the rug . . . (*Tries to make light of it.*) Don't worry. It won't happen again. It can't happen again. There's no more left. (*Turns the flask upside down.*) See?

The flask is not empty. The rest of the whisky spills on the rug. Leslie screams.

Jesus . . . It sure felt empty.

Leslie begins to move towards the kitchen. Ben quickly moves past her, stopping her.

No, I'll do it. You spill something, you wipe it up. That's all there is to it. I keep my rags under the sink. Where do you keep yours? (*moving to exit and pointing*) The kitchen? It's this way, right?

Leslie What?

Ben Don't worry. I'll find it. (*Exits.*)

Arthur begins pacing back and forth. Leslie follows him. They talk in harsh whispers while Ben is out of the room.

Arthur That guy is fucking unreal!

Leslie I know he is. But he lives on the same street.

Arthur Why'd I have to pick this street?

Leslie Why? Because you couldn't live without this house, that's why.

Arthur Who is he? What's he doing here?

Leslie He's a neighbour, that's all.

Arthur He's more than a neighbour. He didn't just come here to come here. I mean, he just walks in here. He gets us to play that asshole game. He spills brandy all over my sleeve. If it doesn't come out, that's nineteen hundred bucks down the goddamn drain. And now he spills booze on the rug. Eighty-seven hundred dollars, and he acts like it came from Sears. How'd he ever get in here? Why didn't you just ask him to leave?

Leslie Me? You opened the door. You let him walk in here.

Arthur I figured it'd be five minutes. I didn't know it was going to be all night. Why'd you take his coat?

Leslie What else was I supposed to do? He was just standing there.

Arthur I want him out of this house.

Leslie Arthur, we can't avoid him. He's five doors down. He knows everybody in the neighbourhood. He knows everything about them. We hardly know anybody. We've met the Melbournes. We've met him. That's it. There's a lot of important people on this block. What if he tells them we threw him out of our house?

Arthur What important people?

Leslie Martin Goodman. He's a vice president at Campbell-Ewald. David and Marilyn Gendich. They own Keystone Mat. Michael Hayes. He runs Motor Insurance. John Cates. He works for Burroughs. (*Gestures towards the kitchen.*) And he probably knows them all, Arthur.

Arthur (*pause*) How'd you find out about them?

Leslie Barbara Melbourne told me. You were out looking at their Mercedes.

Arthur (*frustrated*) What am I supposed to do? The guy drives me crazy.

Leslie Control yourself, that's all. Just be nice to him. Twenty, thirty minutes. You can charm anybody. I've seen you do it. We don't have to invite him over again. And if he invites us over, we can always get out of it.

Arthur All right . . . twenty minutes.

Leslie Just make him feel comfortable. Get him a beer. That's all you've got to do.

Arthur (*putting an arm around her*) All right.

Leslie (*kisses him*) That's my Arthur.

Ben re-enters from the kitchen carrying a large wad of wet paper towels.

Ben I couldn't find any rags. (*holding up the paper towels*) Is this all right?

Arthur (*smiling*) What in the hell are you doing, Ben?

Ben I'm going to clean up the vodka.

Arthur Ben, you're a guest.

Leslie moves to Ben and takes the wad of paper towels. Arthur moves past Ben, pats him on the shoulder, and exits into the kitchen.

Leslie (*taking the paper towels*) Here, Ben, let me do it.

Ben No, I spilled it. I'll clean it up.

Leslie (*kneeling and sponging the whisky spots on the rug*) I know how to do it.

Ben It's not that hard. I do it at home all the time.

Leslie (*glances up*) You do?

Ben (*pause. Picks up his flask, recaps it*) It's about that time, isn't it? (*Slips the flask back into his pocket.*) It's getting late . . . It is late.

Leslie (*standing up and moving towards the kitchen*) It's not that late. And we really haven't had a chance to talk to you.

Arthur re-enters carrying a six-pack of Carlsberg beer, an opener, and a crystal beer glass. Leslie exits into the kitchen with the wad of used paper-towels.

Arthur (*setting the six-pack on top of a magazine on the coffee table*) Leslie's right, Ben. You live down the street. We've just met you. We hardly know anything about you. We don't even know what you do. It's time to relax. Get to know each other. Besides, I thought you were looking for a good time tonight.

Ben I was . . .

Arthur (*picking up a bottle of beer and holding it*) Look, we're going to be living together on the same street. We're going to be passing each other on the weekends. We don't want to start out by fighting over a goddamn rug, do we?

Ben No, that wouldn't be a good way to start out . . .

Leslie re-enters with a bottle of club soda and another wad of clean paper towels. She moves to the spill on the rug, kneels down, pours a small amount of club soda on it, and then begins to sponge it with the paper towels.

Arthur It was an accident. Just like my sleeve. You didn't do it on purpose, did you?

Ben No, I didn't do it on purpose.

Arthur Then there's nothing to worry about, is there?

Ben No . . .

Leslie (*standing up*) You can't even see it, Ben.

Ben If you have to take it to the cleaners, I'll pay for it.

Leslie It came right out. We don't have to take it to the cleaners. (*Exits with the bottle of club soda and the used paper towels.*)

Arthur It's bound to happen, Ben. Have you ever been to somebody's house where it didn't happen? (*Opens the bottle of beer and pours part of it into the crystal beer glass.*)

Ben No. I've seen it happen a lot of times. I went to a party once, I saw a guy knock over a punch bowl. There was pineapple all over the place. Strawberries. Watermelon. Grapes. Cherries. Peach balls. Cantaloupe balls.

Arthur Exactly. (*Arthur hands the glass of beer to Ben.*) Here you go.

Ben Thanks. (*admiring*) That's a beautiful glass.

Arthur Yes, it is. And it's part of a set.

Ben (*grasping the glass with both hands*) Part of a set . . . Right . . .

Arthur You know, it's really important, Ben.

Ben What's that?

Arthur Starting out right. (*Arthur puts an arm around Ben's shoulder, gripping it.*) The reason I was thinking about it, I remember when I was a kid, fifteen, this real overweight guy, Ernie Leadbetter, he moved into the neighbourhood, three doors down. We were living on Joy Road.

Ben (*uncomfortable*) Joy Road . . . Right . . .

Leslie re-enters from the kitchen. She stands near the kitchen hallway and watches Arthur and Ben.

Arthur This guy Leadbetter, he didn't do anything except take care of his lawn. He'd be out there, eight o'clock at night with a flashlight, weeding it. You know how some people get. Certain things are really important to them. Certain things mean more to them than other things.

Ben Sure . . .

Arthur Like lawns. Like cars. Like houses. Those kinds of things.

Ben Right . . . I've got this one T-shirt . . . Black . . . It doesn't even fit any more . . . Its got a hole in one of the armpits . . . But I can't get myself to throw it out. It's got Steve McQueen on it . . .

Arthur Exactly. And if somebody threw it out, then you'd go looking for them, wouldn't you?

Ben I don't know if I'd do that . . . Not over a T-shirt . . . At least not at night . . .

Arthur But some guys might do it, right? I mean, if it meant that much to them . . .

Ben Some guys might do it . . . I know a couple of guys who might do it . . . This guy I know, Charlie Aldridge, he might do it . . .

Arthur Well, I know I'd do it, Ben. No doubt about it. That's just the way I am. Anyway, this friend of mine, Randy Fields, he rode his bike over Leadbetter's front lawn. Leadbetter grabbed him, right off his bike, made him put his right hand on the grass, made him spread his fingers, and then he stepped on them.

Ben Jesus . . .

Leslie He really did that?

Arthur (*nods*) He broke Randy's middle finger. Ernie was a hefty guy. Randy's old man, Big Johnny, Randy's brother, Dave, and me, we went out that night with shovels and dug up Leadbetter's front lawn. All of it. Including the tulips. I always remember Ernie Leadbetter the next day, the look on his face, sitting on his steps, staring out at his front lawn, or what was left of it, holding a Budweiser and a broken tulip.

Ben He must have been real depressed . . . Something that important to him . . . All the work that went into it . . .

Arthur (*nods*) Yeah, he didn't look like he was up for a party. (*Slowly removes his arm from around Ben's shoulder. Simply*) But see, Ernie didn't start out right.

Ben No, he didn't . . .

Arthur All he had to do was start out right, and it never would have happened.

Ben No, it wouldn't have . . .

Arthur Ernie could have made a lot of friends in the neighbourhood, even been one of the guys, maybe even played Friday-night poker, but he just couldn't get that lawn out of his mind.

Ben (*pause*) What'd Ernie do about his lawn?

Arthur Nothing. He just moved.

Ben nods. He glances at Leslie and forces a smile. She smiles back at him. He turns back to Arthur and forces a smile.

Ben He moved? I think we're going to be friends, Arthur.

Arthur (*picking up his brandy and smiling*) No reason not to be, Ben.

They all drink.

Blackout.

Act Two

Lights. No passage of time. Ben is drinking his beer. Arthur and Leslie haven't moved. Ben stops drinking his beer. He glances at Arthur and Leslie, then between them, and then down at the rug. He steps over the wet part of the rug and moves away from it.

Ben (*holds up his beer*) You know, I used to be able to pour a case down, twenty-four bottles, and then some, every night, when I was twenty-one, twenty-two, building part of the Penn-Lincoln Highway out of Pittsburgh. And then I'd be up by six the next morning, driving to work by six-thirty. Iron City beer. You can't get it around here. They only make it in Pittsburgh. (*Shakes his head.*) Iron City – you could taste it for a week.

Arthur Ben?

Ben What?

Arthur What do you do now?

Ben Me?

Leslie What do you do for a living?

Arthur You've got to do something, don't you?

Ben Sure . . .

Leslie You've got a house in Birmingham, right?

Ben Right . . .

Arthur You've got a wife. You've got kids. You've got to support them. You've got to make money.

Ben I make money. I support everybody . . . (*Looks around the living room.*) I'm kind of embarrassed, that's all . . .

Leslie About what?

Ben It's pretty ordinary. It's not the law. It's not teaching. It's nothing like that. Most guys could do it . . .

Arthur Ben, it doesn't matter. You're a neighbour. We'd just like to know what you do, that's all. Wouldn't we?

Leslie We would.

Ben (*staring at his glass of beer*) I'm a fireman.

Leslie I knew it had to be something like that.

Ben How'd you know?

Leslie (*slight pause, looks to Arthur*) You've got the build, that's all. Doesn't he?

Arthur He's got the build.

Ben It's a lot of hard work . . .

Arthur How many fires have you put out, anyway?

Ben Jesus, I don't know . . . You lose count. Fifteen hundred. Maybe two thousand.

Leslie What's the biggest fire you ever put out?

Ben Last week . . . Tuesday night . . . A place called the Rosemont Hotel. I got my name in the *Free Press*. I pulled a woman out.

Arthur (*to Leslie*) That's why he was asking us about the *Free Press*. (*to Ben*) Right?

Ben Right . . .

Leslie (*to Arthur*) Last Wednesday . . . I think I read the *Free Press*. (*to Ben*) I didn't read all of it.

Ben They kind of buried it. Page forty-two, bottom of the page, left-hand corner, right next to a Midas Muffler ad. They didn't place it right. Most people never look at the bottom left-hand corner, even if it's page two. But it happened late. The *Free Press* was already rolling, so I'm lucky it got in at all. The *News*, they just listed it as another fire. No story. No nothing.

Arthur Ben?

Ben What?

Arthur Why didn't you just tell us who you were?

Leslie (*to Arthur*) I don't understand it either.

Ben The thing is, I wanted to, when I first came in, but if I start talking about it, most people, they don't want to listen. They've got their own lives. They're busy people. Like you people. I knew that right off.

Arthur I wouldn't mind hearing about it. What about you?

Leslie I wouldn't mind either.

Ben You really want to hear about it?

Arthur I've always been fascinated by fires.

Leslie So have I.

Arthur I even burned down our garage when I was eight.

Leslie You burned down a garage?

Arthur (*shrugging*) We were living in Dearborn. It was an accident. Nobody got hurt. The car was in the driveway.

Leslie How come you never told me about it?

Arthur I forgot.

Leslie How could you forget about burning down an entire garage?

Arthur I was eight years old, all right? I was playing with the old man's lighter.

Leslie Arthur, if you were playing around with your father's lighter, then it couldn't have been an accident.

Arthur (*irritated*) It was an accident. I lit some wax paper by mistake.

Leslie How could you light wax paper by mistake?

Arthur I wanted to see how fast it'd burn, that's all.

Ben Look, if you don't want to hear the story, that's okay.

Arthur and Leslie glance at Ben, both realising that they had forgotten about him.

I mean, I wouldn't want you people to get bored or anything.

Arthur (*glances at Leslie, then at Ben, smiles*) You're a hero, Ben.

Leslie (*picking it up*) You saved a woman.

Arthur How could we possibly get bored?

Ben It's a pretty exciting story . . .

Leslie I'm sure it is.

Ben I wouldn't tell it if it wasn't. I've got a lot of other stories.

Arthur pours the rest of the beer into Ben's glass.

Leslie (*as Arthur pours*) I'll bet you do.

Arthur So, let's get into it.

Leslie What happened at the . . .

Ben Rosemont.

Leslie That's right, the Rosemont.

Arthur How'd you get your name in the *Free Press*?

Arthur and Leslie sit down next to each other on the couch. Arthur puts an arm around Leslie's shoulders. Ben takes a quick sip of beer, and then sets the bottle down.

Ben Like I said, it was last Tuesday night, eleven-nineteen, that's when the alarm came in. A real firetrap, the Rosemont, mostly welfare people, every one of them black. Anyway, the Rosemont was a real scorcher. You could see it for twenty blocks. You could smell it for thirty. It took eight hours for the complete put-out. Most guys don't come out of a place like the Rosemont. Not without burns. Not without heart attacks. It had to be eleven hundred, twelve hundred degrees in there. Wires jumping and popping. And the smoke was so thick, you couldn't see five inches in front of you. Two inches maybe. But once I got inside, I stayed close to the wall and felt my way up the stairs.

Arthur It must have been some trip.

Ben Scary, let me tell you.

Leslie (*to Arthur*) I can understand why he was scared. (*Leans forward, to Ben.*) That's one thing I can understand.

Ben I wasn't that scared. You know, just normal scared. You make fear work for you, that's all. I wasn't terrified or anything like that, not like a lot of guys would have been. I remember my heart pumping like it was going to break out of my chest. In fact, the fire was so bad, a half an hour after we got there the commander shifted into a defensive mode.

Arthur A defensive mode?

Ben You just pull back. Nobody goes into the place. I guess it looked like it might flash over. You know, just explode. You get caught in a flash-over, that's it. Just rolls over you. Turns you into fuel. No way you can get out of it unless you know how to fly. So, we pulled back and just kept pouring water on it. But that's when I spotted her. She was in the window for a second, and then she was gone. So, I disobeyed the commander's orders and ran inside. Right up to the third floor.

Arthur You disobeyed orders? Hey, that's pretty serious, Ben.

Ben Look, I knew what had to be done, okay?

Leslie Did you have an oxygen tank?

Ben I had a Scott air-pack. There wasn't enough time for a full pack. It gave out on the way down. I had to hold my breath.

Arthur Why didn't you just toss up a ladder to get her out?

Ben I told you. It was a defensive mode.

Arthur That's right. You weren't supposed to go in there.

Leslie (*to Ben*) Besides, it was eleven hundred, twelve hundred degrees, right?

Arthur I forgot.

Leslie The building could have exploded.

Arthur I said I forgot.

Ben I thought I was telling this story.

Leslie I'm sorry, Ben.

Ben You two are just like my wife. So, anyway, I got up to the third floor and kicked down the door.

Arthur Because you didn't have your axe, right?

Ben Right. What else was I supposed to do?

Arthur I'm just verifying it, that's all.

Leslie Was the door locked?

Ben The door? How should I know?

Leslie Well, you were there, weren't you?

Ben What do you mean? Of course I was there. What is this, anyway? I put my life on the line, risk a flash-over, get up there, bring her down, most of the ceiling collapsing, and you're worried about what goddamn door it was. Look, it was an important night, okay? It was the most important night of my life, and if you don't want to listen to it, really listen to it, just let me know.

Arthur (*pause, glances at Leslie*) I think what Leslie's trying to get at, Ben, it just seems like it would have been a lot harder to kick in a locked door, that's all.

Ben God almighty, it was on fire. It was half-gone when I got to it.

Leslie How'd you know which door it was?

Ben I remembered the window where she was screaming.

Arthur How'd you get her out of there?

Ben Dragged her.

Arthur That's it?

Ben That's what you're supposed to do.

Arthur (*to Leslie*) I thought it'd be more complicated.

Ben Dragging. It's basic. You might even have to crawl. Sometimes you've even got to knock them out.

Leslie Did you use the stairs?

Ben The stairs? Of course I did.

Arthur How come you didn't use the fire escape?

Ben The fire escape . . . It was starting to rip out.

Leslie Why didn't you just drop her into one of those nets?

Ben (*irritated*) Christ, I don't know! (*Looks away, then back.*) Sure I do. Now I remember. What was it? She was screaming. That's right. She was hysterical.

Arthur I figured she'd be unconscious. All that smoke.

Ben Yeah, that's what I figured, too. But she must have found an air pocket. I never got a chance to ask her.

Arthur Well, if she was screaming, why didn't you just knock her out?

Ben You can't knock her out and then push her out the window.

Leslie You can't do that, Arthur.

Ben It'd be murder.

Leslie Exactly.

Ben Besides, as soon as she knew I was there, she stopped screaming.

Arthur (*leans back*) It's amazing. (*to Leslie*) Isn't it amazing?

Ben What's amazing?

Arthur What's amazing? I can't get over it. Listen to this guy. Ben, you drag a woman down three flights of stairs . . .

Leslie (*competing*) You can't see . . . What? Two, three inches in front of you.

Arthur (*leaning towards Leslie*) It's eleven hundred, twelve hundred degrees . . .

Leslie Any second the whole building might collapse . . .

Arthur Or flash over . . .

Leslie Or both.

Arthur But you make it out.

Leslie You live to tell the story.

Arthur I mean, Ben, come on now.

Leslie That's amazing.

Arthur They ought to make a movie out of it.

Leslie It'd make a wonderful movie, Ben.

Ben You think so?

Arthur Definitely.

Leslie (*to Arthur*) Jack Nicholson as Ben. (*to Ben*) How's that sound?

Ben Great. Except he doesn't really look like me. Does he?

Arthur (*to Ben*) You're right. Jack Nicholson's all wrong.

Leslie Then who?

Ben (*quickly*) Steven McQueen? (*realising*) No . . .

Arthur Somebody like Clint Eastwood.

Leslie (*to Ben*) I hate Clint Eastwood.

Ben I kind of like his movies . . .

Arthur So do I. *Dirty Harry*.

Ben (*nods*) *The Enforcer.*

Arthur *Magnum Force.*

Ben (*a bit faster*) *Sudden Impact.*

Arthur (*a bit faster*) *The Gauntlet.*

Ben (*faster, competing*) *Hang 'Em High*!

Arthur (faster, competing) *Escape From Alcatraz*!

Ben *Fistful of Dollars*!

Arthur *For a Few Dollars More*!

Ben *and* **Arthur** (*trying to outshout each other*) *The Good, the Bad, and the Ugly*!

Leslie (*putting her hands over her ears and screaming*) Stop it! (*Takes her hands away from her ears, somewhat embarrassed.*) All he ever does is shoot people. Or maim them. It's not normal, Arthur.

Arthur (*studies Leslie, shakes his head 'no'*) No, it has to be Clint Eastwood, Ben. He's the only one around who could do what you did and make it look real.

Leslie I can't understand the attraction. I never will.

Ben (*picks up his beer, sips it*) Wouldn't that be something? Somebody like Clint Eastwood . . . It was pretty incredible, I guess, the Rosemont . . .

Arthur Pretty incredible?

Leslie It was incredible period.

Ben Thanks . . . Thanks a lot. And you know what else?

Arthur What's that, Ben?

Ben The lieutenant, he really jumped all over me for disobeying the commander's orders. Grabbed me, threw me up against a truck, told me he was going to bring me up before a hearing, throw the book at me.

Leslie You're kidding. You?

Arthur Hey, I can understand, you disobeyed orders, but you brought her out, right? That's got to count, doesn't it?

Ben Not to the lieutenant. But he didn't see her in the window, that's all. Nobody did. That's why they went into a defensive mode. No, he wanted to boot me. Right on the spot. Even though the whole crowd was cheering. Toasting me with wine bottles. Clapping. Cheering. Dancing around. Banging on car hoods. Radios blaring. And the next day, when the *Free Press* came out, when I had my name in print, the lieutenant, he didn't say a word to me. Not a word. It was like he hadn't even been at the fire. He knew . . . He knew all I had to do was call up the guy from the *Free Press* who interviewed me, Jerry Giordano. He knew. (*He reaches into an inside jacket pocket, takes out the* Free Press *tearsheet, and unfolds it, part of 'his' article has been clipped off in the middle of the story.*) I thought you might like to see it. I mean, after hearing me tell the story and everything.

Ben hands the tearsheet to Arthur. Arthur shares it with Leslie.

Arthur (*taking it*) Sure, Ben.

Leslie Bottom left-hand corner.

Ben Right.

Arthur What happened to the rest of it?

Ben (*forces a laugh*) The rest of it was about everybody else. The fire getting put out. I didn't need it.

Leslie (*pointing*) There it is.

Arthur (*nodding*) Benjamin A. Cook.

Leslie (*to Ben*) Without the 'e'.

Ben I made sure he spelled it right.

Arthur You know what would have been nice?

Ben What's that?

Arthur A picture.

Leslie It would have been.

Ben The guy who interviewed me, Jerry Giordano, he said they didn't need a picture. But I sent him a Polaroid, anyway. Just in case. Standing in front of my house with my dress uniform on. Walt Wagner took it.

Arthur Your next-door neighbour, right?

Ben Right. I think he'd been drinking. He took five shots, and they all came out fuzzy. I thought they might want to do a follow-up story. They do that a lot of times, and the guy's a good writer . . . (*pointing to the tearsheet*) You can tell, right?

Leslie He's very clear . . .

Ben At least he put my name in the second paragraph. He could have waited for the fourth paragraph. But I haven't heard from him yet. Maybe I'll get a call tomorrow. No, tomorrow's Sunday. Maybe Monday.

Arthur (*hands the tearsheet back to Ben*) That's a pretty big muffler ad, Ben. It must have cost them ten thousand.

Ben That's what I said when I saw it. If they'd run it on Thursday, I might have made the upper-right-hand corner . . . (*He folds the tearsheet and puts it back into his inside jacket pocket.*)

Leslie If I were you, Ben, I'd get it framed.

Ben I don't need to get it framed. I've got a copy on the kitchen wall, and one in the bathroom. Plus this one.

That's enough. (*Nods, smiles.*) It's nice to meet people who understand.

Leslie Thank you, Ben.

Ben That's something most of the guys around the station don't do. (*Pause.*) There wasn't any party on Quarton. There was a party at Bill Palmer's house out around Indian Village, but I wasn't invited. I thought most of them were close friends. I've known a lot of them fourteen, fifteen years. I thought those guys'd die for me. But it could have been tense, a bunch of guys from the station.

Arthur How come?

Ben (*forcing a smile*) See, I just about creamed a guy today because he was talking behind my back, imitating me, putting down the Rosemont, calling me a 'freelancer'. Me. A 'FREELANCER'. Because I went against orders in a 'defensive mode'. But the commander walked in, and well, things didn't go too well after that . . .

Leslie What happened?

Ben (*forcing a smile*) Lost my job. Fired me. Right in front of the whole crew. I thought a couple of the guys might defend me, but they just stared at the floor. I could maybe appeal it, but it's hard to go up against the commander. (*Pause.*) It might have been different if things had worked out . . .

Arthur Come on, Ben, you're protected. You've got the *Free Press* on your side.

Leslie Of course you do. That reporter who interviewed you . . .

Ben (*nods*) Yeah. Jerry Giordano. Nice guy.

Leslie Jerry Giordano. He knows what you did.

Arthur Sure he does.

Ben (*nods, smiles*) That was some night, the Rosemont. Some night . . . They were going to let her burn up . . . They were . . . (*He nods, staring straight ahead.*)

Leslie glances at Arthur, both of them slightly uncomfortable.

Leslie Ben?

Arthur (*pause*) Ben?

Ben takes the tearsheet out of his inside jacket pocket, starts to unfold it, starts to hand it to Arthur, suddenly realises what he is doing, and then puts the tearsheet back into his pocket, picking up his beer.

Ben (*as he does so*) What?

Leslie (*glances at Arthur, then at Ben, forcing a smile*) How long have you been a fireman?

Ben Twenty-one years.

Arthur You've been a fireman for twenty-one years?

Ben Twenty-one years . . . That's right.

Arthur (*to Leslie*) I don't know anybody who's been at the same job for twenty-one years.

Leslie My father worked at Ford's for thirty-five years.

Arthur He was trapped, that's why.

Leslie Arthur, he wasn't trapped.

Arthur Like hell he wasn't. (*to Ben*) Christ, he's still living on Six Mile and Evergreen.

Ben (*nods*) Six Mile and Evergreen . . . That's a pretty rough area. Ladder truck got stoned around there last year.

Leslie (*to Ben*) They like the house, that's all.

Ben (*nods*) Lots of nice houses in Palmer Park. I hear you can pick them up for a dime. Five, six bedrooms. It's too bad they're not out here.

Arthur (*to Leslie*) Come on, it went black twenty-five years ago. (*to Ben*) Now it's got Arabs buying up two blocks at a time. The Lebanese are walking all over the blacks.

Ben That's what I hear . . .

Arthur (*to Leslie*) And your parents are still there. Nobody likes a house that much. (*to Ben, about Leslie's father*) Guy wanted to be an engineer, but ended up a foreman. That's why he's still there.

The exchange between Leslie and Arthur is calm and polite, each of them trying to control their irritation.

Leslie (*setting her wine glass down*) And what about your father, Arthur? A ninth-grade biology teacher. What's that?

Arthur Well, at least he didn't get drunk all the time and go around punching my face out just because the linoleum wasn't shined.

Leslie Arthur, your father couldn't even afford the payments on his fifty-six Plymouth. Remember?

Arthur It was a bad time for him, that's all.

Leslie (*to Ben*) And it was one of the 'Low Price Three'.

Ben Right . . . I remember the 'Low Price Three'.

Arthur (*trying to control his anger*) Look, I got away from it, didn't I? I didn't settle for the Parks Department like my brother, did I? I don't live next to a bunch of Arabs, do I?

Ben (*diverting the argument*) You know, they had this Dalmatian when I first joined up. That's how far back I go. Charlie Chaser. That's what we called him. Real friendly. Real fast. Charlie Chaser was so fast, sometimes he'd been waiting for us when we got to the fire. He'd just keep ahead of the truck.

Leslie (*picking up her wine glass, still irritated*) What happened to Charlie Chaser?

Ben He got run over.

Arthur (*still irritated*) Well, at least it was in the line of duty.

Ben No, some drunk hit him outside the station one night when Charlie was taking a crap – (*to Leslie*) Excuse me.

Leslie That's all right . . .

Ben It just kind of slipped out . . .

Leslie I understand . . .

Ben Anyway, that was the end of Charlie Chaser. They never bothered to replace him. The funniest thing, I still miss him. He loved rubbing against your right knee, Charlie Chaser . . .

Leslie You can really get attached to Dalmatians, can't you?

Leslie sets her wine glass down. Ben and Arthur, reacting to her last remark, slowly turn and stare at her.

Arthur (*turning back to Ben*) Is that what you always wanted to be, Ben? A fireman?

Ben No . . . What I mean, it's a good life. It's decent money. It's regular. You never run out of fires. I had a few other jobs before I joined the department. I worked for Bethlehem Steel for three years, right after I got bounced out of the army. (*Forces a smile.*) I could have made it in the army, maybe even been a first sergeant, if I hadn't decked a captain in Frankfurt, fighting for my rights, except nobody cared about them.

Arthur Hey, Ben, the army, it's no big thing.

Ben Yeah, no big thing. (*Pause.*) I must have dreamed about that captain for ten years. And I never took the swing. Not once. Anyway, right after the army, I started moving around. Construction work. Tending bar. I even drove an airport bus for nine months. I was living in Cleveland. Until I drove to the wrong airport once. (*Pause.*) But see, what I really wanted to do, and I could have done it, except . . . No, it doesn't matter any more.

Arthur What'd you want to do, Ben?

Leslie I'd like to hear about it.

Ben I wanted to play ball. That's what I really wanted to do. I was one hell of a football player in my time. I was. Going into senior year, I was All City and All State. I've still got a couple of records posted behind glass. You know, I used to walk down hallways, and nobody clicked a locker. And let me tell you, they really played a rough brand of football in Pittsburgh.

Leslie Arthur played football in high school. They won the city championship.

Ben Is that right? Where'd you play?

Arthur Here.

Ben Detroit?

Arthur Pershing Doughboys.

Ben I hate to tell you, Arthur, but Detroit's nothing compared to Pittsburgh ball.

Arthur (*pause*) No?

Ben Hell, no. (*Pats Arthur's shoulder.*) No offence. Really. It's just a fact.

Arthur Just a fact, huh?

Leslie I was a Doughboy cheerleader. I went to all the games, Ben. You really don't know what you're talking about. Arthur had his jaw broken twice.

Ben (*to Leslie*) Twice? (*to Arthur*) Is that all?

Arthur Ben, here you played against black kids, right off a truck from Alabama. Here you played against hillbillies, their fathers got jobs screwing on door handles at River Rouge. Here you played against Polocks, Hamtramck Polocks. Shit, they didn't even speak English. The Warsaw Warriors. That's what we called them. And they weren't seventeen, eighteen years old either. Most of them were in their goddamn twenties.

Leslie They came for jobs, or they came here to play football. Everybody knew that. They came to Detroit to get noticed, didn't they?

Arthur (*nods*) They handed you a number, or they handed you a drill.

Ben Maybe they did. But in Pittsburgh you played against giants, kids who worked in the steel mills. Kids who poured iron during the summers. Kids who looked like barrels. Kids who felt like cement, necks this big, shoulders that wide, all of them six foot and up, all of them two hundred, two hundred and fifty pounds. This one guard from McKeesport, he was three hundred and ten. You know what it's like to slam into three hundred and ten pounds? No, of course you don't. You never had to do it in Detroit, did you?

Arthur Big doesn't mean shit. Here they carried razor blades up their sleeves.

Ben Well, see, the thing about Pittsburgh, they didn't need razors. Their fingernails were twice as sharp. They never cut them. They just left them in your throat. And they wore brass knuckles, all taped over.

Arthur It wasn't any different here, except they didn't tape them. As long as you won, that's all that counted. 'Just bring home the dream,' that's what they used to chant.

Leslie (*remembering, smiles*) Right . . . 'Just bring home the dream' . . . (*getting excited*) Remember that McKenzie game?

Arthur (*nods*) I remember it.

Leslie (*getting more excited*) You and Bill Peters.

Arthur (*catching the excitement, to Ben*) Pouring goddamn rain. Twelve seconds left, and I connected with the son of a bitch. I couldn't even see him. (*to Leslie*) I had a tackle and two guards hanging onto me –

Leslie (*nods*) I remember it.

Arthur (to *Ben*) Two of them were trying to rip off my helmet. (*to Leslie*) I didn't even know I'd connected till I heard the crowd. Mud all over my face. Spitting blood. Three guys on top of me. (*Grins.*) What a sound!

Leslie Everybody pouring out of the bleachers, hanging all over the goalposts . . .

Arthur (*to Ben*) A rocket. That's what it was. A rocket!

Leslie leans over and takes Arthur's hands, squeezes them.

Leslie Jesus, I loved watching you on the field.

Arthur (*squeezes her hands, nods*) That's when Detroit was a great fucking city!

Leslie (*nods, smiles*) It was.

Ben Yeah, I'm sure it was. But where I played ball, you complained, that's the only way you got tossed out of a game. If you got caught under a pile, you made out your will. The whistle didn't mean anything. They'd punch you in the kidneys, put fingers in your eyes, try to rip off one of your lips, try to carry your tongue back to the huddle, or, pardon me, but he's got to know – (*to Arthur, shows*) – stick their hands all the way down, give them a twist, and then dig in their nails.

Arthur (*amused*) In Detroit, they wouldn't have even felt it.

Ben In Detroit, it would have been like grabbing a couple of pebbles.

Arthur Here they hired gangs to break your legs before the game.

Leslie (*to Arthur*) Remember Tommy Sullivan?

Arthur I remember him. (*to Ben*) They caught this guy, Tommy Sullivan, toughest half-back in the city, he was coming out of the locker room two days before the McKenzie game. They worked him over with baseball bats. They put him in the hospital for seven months. I saw him three years ago at a Red Wings game. He's still got a cane, and he's just about blind in his left eye.

Ben (*leans forward*) All I know is, you weren't in Pittsburgh. I was. When I was busy racking up points, setting Pennsylvania records, you were trotting around Detroit bumping into each other. 'Cookin' with Cook,' that's what they said about me. Hell, I could have played for the Steelers if this one son of a bitch hadn't done a job on my ankle. Busted it wide open. Bone shot up right through my laces. Curtis Cunningham. Every time I think about him, I keep hoping he's working in a car wash. Guy didn't have any talent. He couldn't even block. But he knew how to find a joint, and he knew what to do with it once he'd found it. I wasn't even supposed to play. That's the kicker. I had a pulled tendon. But it was my chance. My chance. The Steelers were sending a scout. My old man came down to the locker room. Almost punched out the coach. Just about dragged me out to the field. Kept yelling at me. The Pittsburgh Steelers were sending a scout to check me out. Didn't I know what that meant? (*Pause.*) They would have taken me right out of high school, that's how good I was, Arthur. I could have been coaching at Ohio State by now.

Arthur Look, Ben, I'm sure it's a very touching story, but –

Ben No, it's not just a touching story, pal. It's the truth. You want to know what it was really like to lose out in Pittsburgh? My old man . . . That son of a bitch, he stopped talking to me the day I busted my ankle. Used to come to all my games, my old man. Used to hug me up against the lockers when we won. Used to take me over to the Ellsworth Café for a beer after the games. Used to show me off to all his friends. Till I busted my ankle. I came home from the hospital, and he had my bedroom sitting on the front lawn. On the front lawn! Didn't matter that I'd scored thirty-seven touchdowns. Didn't matter that he'd made a couple of thousand bucks betting on me. All my trophies broken . . . I couldn't even find most of the heads . . . That's what it was like in Pittsburgh when you lost out, my friend. (*Shakes his head, fades out for a moment.*) My old man . . . Won himself a purple heart on some beach in Italy way back when . . . Never let me forget it . . . Kept it on the mantelpiece just to remind me . . .

Arthur Well, it's too bad about your trophies, Ben, ending up on the front lawn and everything, except running in Pittsburgh, compared to Detroit, it was like crossing the street. You know, real late at night, no traffic either way, nobody around, and the light on your side.

Ben (*to Leslie*) Pardon me. (*to Arthur*) Bullshit. When it comes to football, you don't know your ass from a hole in the ground. If you'd played ball in Pittsburgh, you wouldn't be here now. No, sir. You'd be sitting in a wheelchair somewhere. Talking through a voice box. That's what you'd be doing.

Arthur Is that a fucking fact, Ben?

Ben (*to Leslie*) Pardon me. (*to Arthur*) That's a fucking fact, mister.

Arthur (*moving very close to Ben*) If you'd played ball in Detroit, Ben, they would have ripped off your fucking head and taken a shit down your neck!

Arthur and Ben stare hard at one another. Ben slowly finishes his beer, keeping his eyes on Arthur, and then casually flips the glass from one hand to the other, setting it down on the coffee table, never taking his eyes off Arthur.

Ben All right, fella, why don't we find out who's right?

Arthur What do you mean, find out who's right?

Ben Simple. Why don't I just run against you?

Arthur You? Run against me?

Leslie Here?

Ben Sure. I play offence. You play defence. That'd settle the argument, wouldn't it?

Leslie It's a house, for God's sake!

Ben It's a space, that's all it is.

Leslie In case you haven't noticed, it's a living room! Our living room!

Ben We'll just move the furniture out of the way. Give him all the field he needs to catch me.

Leslie He's crazy, Arthur. Don't even consider it.

Ben I'm putting it on the line, that's all I'm doing. If you want to back off, fine, back off. It's a challenge, that's all it is.

Leslie All right, you almost made the Pittsburgh Steelers. You were All City and All State. How's that? (*to Arthur*) I don't want anything broken in this house.

Arthur (*continues to stare at Ben, and then slowly takes off his suit jacket*) Twenty bucks, Ben. One-on-one. Best out of three.

Leslie You can't be serious . . .

Arthur I'm serious. (*He begins moving the furniture out of the way, creating a running space.*)

Leslie What about your suit?

Arthur Fuck my suit.

Leslie Arthur, it's an Armani. You still owe nine hundred dollars on it.

Ben Look, I was just kidding, pal.

Leslie See, he was just kidding.

Ben Really. I just wanted to see if you'd do it, that's all. I'll bet you were pretty good in your day. Detroit's got a reputation. I know that. (*rubbing it in*) We just had different standards in Pittsburgh.

Arthur One-on-one, Ben. Best out of three.

Leslie Arthur, you're not really going to do this.

Arthur I'm going to break that pussy in half, that's what I'm going to do!

Leslie This is insane . . .

Arthur I played tough fucking ball in this city! Four years of it! You think I'm going to let this asshole walk all over me?!

Leslie Then do it tomorrow.

Arthur I've got to work tomorrow. I've got the Heller contracts tomorrow.

Ben I told you. I was just kidding.

Arthur (*to Ben*) Then you shouldn't have brought it up, right?

Ben Look, you've got a real nice living room. Real Italian. You don't want to fall down all over it.

Arthur You going to run against me or not?

Leslie You're supposed to be adults. Who cares if somebody ran faster in Pittsburgh or harder in Detroit? Who really cares? That was high school.

Arthur You cared about it two minutes ago.

Leslie That's when we were talking about it. Not doing it.

Arthur I'm waiting, Ben.

Leslie Arthur . . .

Ben It's a good thing I'm not wearing my cleats, because you'd be digging them out of your face.

Arthur I'm still waiting.

Leslie You haven't played football in seventeen years.

Arthur What's it going to be, Ben?

Leslie (*starts to move a piece of furniture back into place*) Arthur, I forbid it.

Arthur (*moving towards her*) You forbid it? What's that mean? (*He puts a hand on the piece of furniture, stopping her from moving it.*)

Leslie It doesn't have to be tonight, Arthur. You could do it during the week. You could do it outside. That's where you're supposed to play football. Outside, Arthur.

Ben (*to Arthur*) She's got a point. Hitting the ground, that's a lot better than hitting the floor.

Arthur (*tosses a throw-pillow at Ben's feet*) I don't plan on hitting the floor, Ben.

Leslie Eight hundred and sixty thousand dollars, just about the rest of our lives – (*gesturing around at the house*) – and you don't even respect it, do you?

Arthur I pay for it, don't I? Just about everything I make goes into it, doesn't it? That means I respect it, right? I gave up the Porsche 928S to get the house, didn't I? (*pointing to the throw-pillow*) So, what's it going to be, Ben? You want to see if you can roam just as well in Detroit? Or maybe you're just wide open when the city's right.

Ben They don't play football in this town. They never did. They play ballet.

Arthur Twenty bucks says different, Ben.

Leslie (*to Ben*) Don't do it.

Ben It's a challenge.

Leslie You don't play football in a house!

Arthur That's right, Ben. It's a challenge. That's all it is. What are you going to do about it? Back down? Chicken out? Beg off? You do that, Ben, it's going to make me wonder about all those trophies sitting on the front lawn.

Ben (*stares hard at Arthur, slowly takes off his suit jacket*) You're on, fella. Offence? I carry the ball?

Arthur That's okay. I play defence too.

Leslie Goddamn it, Arthur. Somebody could get hurt.

Arthur Stay out of it, all right?

Leslie You wanted this house. You had to have it. And now it's not even important to you. Right?

Arthur Right now, this is more important.

Leslie Then why'd we even move out here? Nothing was supposed to be more important than this.

Arthur (*limbering up*) You want to live in Detroit? You want to get burned out on Halloween? You want to get shot at on New Year's Eve? You want to buy crack in the A & P? Fine! Move back!

Leslie (*frustrated, looking at the furniture*) Damn it, Arthur, do you know how much time I've put into this house?

Arthur Nothing's going to get broken. Except maybe Ben.

Ben (*limbering up*) I wouldn't count on it, pal.

Leslie (*moving away from the running area*) Children! Five-year-olds!

Arthur (*dragging a foot, setting an upstage goal line*) Pittsburgh, Ben.

Ben (*dragging a foot, setting a downstage goal line*) Detroit, Arthur.

Arthur (*moving downstage, passing Ben*) Think you can make it?

Ben (*moving upstage, passing Arthur*) Piece of cake.

Leslie (*going to the staircase*) I'm going to bed, Arthur.

Ben I wouldn't do that if I were you. He's going to need somebody to wake him up.

Arthur Words, Benny. Let's see what you can really do.

Leslie (*starting up the stairs*) When you two get done playing Super Bowl, it'd be nice if (*pointing to the living room*) you'd clean up what's left of it.

Arthur (*irritated*) I'll take care of it, okay?

Leslie Right. You'll take care of it. (*She moves up the stairs and exits.*)

Ben (*tucking the pillow under his arm*) You ready? Or would you like to say a long prayer?

Arthur (*hunching over*) Ready!

Ben On twenty-one?

Arthur (*getting ready*) On twenty-one!

Leslie creeps down the stairs, trying to stay out of sight.

Ben (*as if going through an actual play*) Thirty-six! Eighteen! Forty-nine! Twenty-one!

Ben, imitating broken-field running, charges at Arthur. Arthur charges at Ben, slamming into him. Ben spins away, throwing Arthur off, stiff-arming him at the same time. Arthur falls to the floor as Ben scores a touchdown. Leslie hurries down the stairs and moves to Arthur. Ben parades around the room, tossing the pillow from hand to hand.

Pittsburgh one! Detroit nothing!

Leslie (*to Arthur*) Are you all right?

Ben One more, Arthur! (*moving towards him*) Don't worry. It'll be over fast. You won't feel a thing.

Arthur gets up slowly, shaking Leslie off.

Arthur (*to Leslie, irritated*) I'm all right. (*He takes off his shoes and socks.*)

Ben (*to Leslie, indicating Arthur*) Second-string. Amateur night. I knew it right off.

Leslie He slipped.

Ben Who made him slip?

Leslie I saw him play.

Ben You saw him play in Detroit.

Arthur (*stops rubbing a knee*) I'm going to kill you, Cook.

Ben (*to Leslie*) He's going to kill me, right? What are we doing, Arthur? Playing tough, or talking tough? Because if we're playing tough, and you just gave me your best shot, then I think you ought to know, I was just getting warmed up.

Arthur (*nods*) I'm going to kill you.

Ben (*tosses the pillow up and catches it*) It's only a game, Arthur. We're just having a little fun.

Arthur moves back into position, waving Leslie out of the way.

Leslie (*to Arthur*) Why don't we just stop now? You already banged your knee. What's next?

Arthur (*shakes his head 'no'*) I'm going to fucking kill him!

Ben (*grinning*) Just 'Bring home the dream,' Arthur. Isn't that what they used to say around here?

Arthur (*concentrating*) You ready?

Ben (*casually*) Sure.

Leslie (*moving out of the way, folding her arms angrily*) Shit!

Ben On twenty-one again?

Arthur On twenty-one.

Leslie (*from the sidelines, to Arthur*) You're sure you're all right?

Arthur I'm all right! (*to Ben*) Let's go!

Ben (*shrugs*) Your funeral, pal. (*as if going through an actual play*) Sixty-seven! Thirty-two! Fifty-eight! Fourteen! Twenty-three! Twenty-one!

Ben, imitating broken-field running, charges forward a second time. Arthur charges at Ben. Ben, close to Arthur, fakes to his right, and then spins to his left. Arthur doesn't go for the fake. He smashes into Ben, letting out a scream. He throws his arms around Ben's waist and begins driving him upstage. Leslie suddenly cheers for Arthur, jumping up and down, clapping wildly. Arthur drives Ben into the upstage wall, and then continues to drive him into the wall, screaming each time he does it. Arthur finally releases Ben. He stumbles away from Ben, cheering, his fists raised over his head in triumph. Ben, the wind knocked out of him, drops the pillow and slides down the wall to his knees, panting, his arms wrapped around his stomach.

Arthur (*on releasing Ben*) Detroit! (*moving around the room*) One-all! One-all! One-all! Doughboys! Motor City Champions! Nineteen seventy-one!

Leslie (*runs to Arthur and throws her arms around him; hugging him tightly, shouts*) You looked terrific, Arthur! Terrific!

Arthur lifts her off her feet. They kiss passionately. They rub their hands all over each other's body. It is almost a sexual foreplay. He releases her. She slides down his body, kissing him.

Arthur (*singing their high-school song, quietly, with feeling*) We're from Pershing High School –

Arthur *and* **Leslie** (*singing quietly, with feeling*)
We're full of fight.
Here's to our colours, of maroon and white.
Fight. Fight. Fight.
Here's to all the Doughboys loyal and true . . .

They forget the rest of the words, laughing and hugging each other. Arthur quickly moves to the six-pack, opens a beer, and then takes a long swig of it. Ben slowly gets up, his breath almost back, and then picks up the pillow, leaning against the wall, trying to get the rest of his breath back. Leslie starts to move around the room, never taking her eyes off Arthur, suddenly becoming eighteen years old again and very sexy.

Leslie (*performing her cheers, seductively*)
We've got a team
That's on the beam,
They're really hep to the jive!
So come on, Doughboys,
Skin 'em alive!

Arthur, excited by her sexiness, raises his beer bottle to her, and then bangs the bottom of it on a table, encouraging her. Performing, strutting:

A-well, I saw a grizzly bear
A-walkin' down the street!
I said, a-hey, grizzly bear,
Why the crazy beat?
He said, a-man, what a square,
Don't ya dig the scene?
The Doughboys are a-comin',
And they're really mean!

Leslie ends the cheer with a high jump, her legs spread apart. Arthur moves to her, drapes an arm around her shoulders, and then kisses her hard on the mouth.

Arthur Remember those fucking games?! Remember those fucking games? Remember those fucking guys?!

Leslie (*laughing*) You and fucking Joanne Taylor! That's what I remember!

Arthur Hey, Charlie Tucker ran into her. Guess what she weighs now? A hundred and eighty pounds!

Leslie A hundred and eighty pounds?! Joanne Taylor?! (*Throws her arms around Arthur and hugs him.*) That's wonderful, Arthur!

Ben (*pushing himself off the wall*) You're good . . . You're not bad . . .

Leslie (*kissing Arthur*) He's the best!

Ben You're in great shape . . . You must be . . . Nobody ever pushed me back that far . . .

Leslie Arthur works out five times a week.

Ben That much?

Arthur moves to the six-pack, opens a beer, and then moves back to Ben, handing him the beer. Leslie moves to the upstage wall, inspecting the smudges on the wall.

Arthur (*getting the beer*) Birmingham Athletic.

Ben Birmingham Athletic, huh? That's a real snazzy place. You've got to have credentials, don't you? I pass it all the time. I've probably seen your car there, except they all look alike, don't they?

Arthur (*handing the beer to Ben*) Here you go. Take a hit on this one.

Ben Thanks . . .

Arthur (*squeezes Ben's shoulder*) Hanging tough, Ben! That's what I like to see! Hanging tough!

Leslie (*of the wall, to Ben*) You really banged into it.

Ben It wasn't my idea. I thought I was going the other way.

Leslie (*moving towards the kitchen*) Time out, guys.

Arthur (*waving at the wall*) Leslie, let it go.

Leslie (*exiting*) Arthur, we just had it painted a month ago!

Arthur Half time, Ben.

Ben Sure.

Leslie exits into the kitchen. When she returns, she carries a spray wall cleaner and a cleaning rag and goes to work on the wall.

Arthur You know what I admire most about you, Ben?

Ben No. What?

Arthur You're a professional. Consequences don't mean shit to you, and that's how things get done in this world. Not many guys like us around any more.

Ben Probably not.

Arthur (*points at the door*) The guys I know, they never took a hit like that in their lives.

Leslie exits into the kitchen again. Arthur puts an arm around Ben's shoulder and leads him to the couch; both of them sit down.

Christ, it felt good. Real contact.

Ben That was some time in my life, Arthur.

Arthur It brought it all back, didn't it? The games, the guys, the plays, the crowds. The only thing missing, you can't see the breath in front of your face. All the money in the world, you can't buy memories like that, can you? (*Pause.*) Shifting numbers around fourteen hours a day. That's what I do. I mean, when you really think about it, what's it got to do with anything? Shifting numbers around just to make people money? People who don't even need it. People like fucking Gil Henschel. (*Shrugs.*) But playing ball, that's when I was really alive. All those parties. All those basements. Jim Morrison. Jefferson Airplane. Credence Clearwater. The Stones. All that grass. Joanne Taylor. God, she was gorgeous. (*Looks towards the kitchen.*) She still is.

Arthur and Ben laugh. Ben stands up.

Ben It's real nice, Arthur. All the memories. But I just want you to know, this last time around, I'm going to stomp you.

Leslie re-enters from the kitchen.

Arthur (*to Leslie*) Did you hear that?

Leslie What?

Arthur He's going to stomp me this time.

Leslie It's a good thing he lives so close. (*to Ben*) We won't have to carry your body that far.

Ben I hope he knows a real good orthopaedist. He's going to need one.

Leslie We'll give you his number. As soon as you get out of the hospital, okay?

Arthur 'Cookin' with Cook', right?

Leslie Right!

Ben Hey, what do you think, pal? I was kidding?

Arthur I just put you up against the wall, Ben. You had to be kidding, right?

Ben You want to bet?

Arthur We've got twenty riding on it already.

Ben Then make it twenty more.

Leslie (*instantly*) Take it, Arthur.

Arthur All right, forty bucks.

Leslie Winner take all.

Arthur We'll buy you a wreath, Ben. How's that sound?

Leslie I want to say 'go' this time. (*to Arthur*) On sixteen.

Arthur Sixteen. Right. (*to Ben, pointing at the back of his shirt*) It used to look like a six when we played in the rain.

Leslie (*kicking her shoes off and climbing up on the couch*) Come on! Let's play some ball!

> *Ben and Arthur move back into position, setting down their beer bottles. Ben picks up the pillow again, tucking it under his arm.*

Arthur Ready, Big Ben?

Ben (*taking deep breaths*) Ready. (*to Leslie*) On sixteen, right?

Leslie On sixteen!

Arthur You think we could maybe see some of that fancy footwork this time around?

Ben If I were you, I'd watch real close. It's the last thing you're ever going to see.

Leslie On sixteen!

Leslie (*calling a play*) Twenty-four! A hundred-and-ten! Eighty-seven! A hundred-and-eighteen! Forty-four!

Arthur (*to Leslie*) Come on!

Leslie Sixty-four! Thirty-nine! Sixteen! Get the son of a bitch!

Ben, imitating broken-field running, charges at Arthur, screaming. He charges three times, Arthur throwing him back twice. Leslie jumps off the couch and cheers Arthur. Ben, using Leslie as a shield, pushes her in front of Arthur. Arthur grabs onto one of Ben's legs, Ben falls into the end zone, scoring a touchdown. Ben jumps up, yells, and then spikes the pillow hard on the floor. He begins twirling himself around the room, jumping in the air.

Ben (*shouting*) Two-one! Two-one! Homestead Headers! Pittsburgh's best! Pittsburgh's champs!

Ben moves to Leslie and throws his arms around her. Leslie, suddenly laughing, caught up in Ben's joy, throws her arms around him, hugs him. Arthur moves to a chair, sits down, and begins putting his shoes and socks on again.

Leslie (*as she hugs him*) Incredible, Ben!

Ben twirls her around the room, Leslie laughing as he does it. Ben sets Leslie down on the floor. There is a sudden attraction to Ben, a flush in her face.

Ben 'Cookin' with Cook'! All over again! (*Moves past Arthur.*) Hanging tough, Arthur! Just like you said! Hanging tough!

Ben takes Leslie's hand and begins wandering around the room with her.

I'm back in the ring, baby! (*even more excited*) Know what I'm going to do?

Leslie (*caught up in it, laughs*) What, Ben?

Ben I'm going to start working out again. Goddamn it, I'm going to join Jack La Lanne's. Get some real tone back. (*Drops her hand, wanders by himself.*) Jesus, you get old fast. I can remember summers when I was a kid, I never thought they'd end. Being eighteen, it didn't mean anything. Driving to practice, the top down on my old man's Chevy, the sun all over my face, running patterns in my head, Elvis on the radio, coming in my ears, going out my fingers . . . 'Cookin' with Cook'! (*Pause.*) Being young . . . Being strong . . . Those were the best years of my life . . . (*Excited again, he moves towards Leslie.*) And my son, he's going to be just like I was. Except when he's done with high school, he's going to be lighting up scoreboards all over the country. (*Tosses the pillow in the air.*) I can't wait to tell my wife about this!

Leslie What's your wife's name, Ben?

Ben Gloria. She's a Detroiter. Like you folks. Grew up on the East Side. We're complete opposites. All she needs is a house and a backyard and she's happy. We went out to celebrate tonight, you know, my name in the paper and everything. (*Indicates his suit jacket.*) She gave me the flask. Sterling silver. She had the date of the Rosemont engrave on it. October 7th. I made reservations at the London Chop House. But we had a little fight . . . (*Becomes distant.*) I caused kind of a scene . . . I lost it for a second, that's all . . . Just kind of blacked out . . . I was talking about the Rosemont, you know, my job, and she wasn't really listening. Just kept going over the menu, asking me what things were. (*Pause.*) I think I knocked over a plate . . . They asked us to leave. Just about got into a fight with the manager. (*excited again*) But it's still 'Cookin' with Cook'! Just like it used to be! And that's all that counts!

Arthur (*slowly standing up*) Not bad, Ben.

Leslie (*noticing Arthur almost for the first time*) Are you all right?

Arthur (*grins*) Hey, I'm fine. Got a couple of ribs shifted around, but what the hell. (*to Ben*) I can live with that, right?

Ben (*moves towards Arthur*) You've still got the power, Arthur. I could feel it. I mean, I played against guys who tried out for the Steelers. I played against two guys who made the Colts.

Leslie Well, what are you waiting for? Pay him the money, Arthur.

Arthur (*starts towards his suit jacket*) Sure.

Leslie Forty bucks (*to Ben*), right?

Ben Right. (*to Arthur*) Look, forget it, okay? (*to Leslie*) Really.

Arthur picks up his suit jacket and takes out his wallet.

Arthur A bet's a bet, Ben.

Ben We were just messing around, that's all. I don't need the money.

Arthur Everybody needs money, Ben. You won. I lost. We had money riding on it. Time to collect, right?

Leslie I'm going to have another glass of wine. Anybody else need anything?

Ben Not me.

Leslie Arthur?

Arthur No thanks.

Leslie (*over her shoulder, exiting to kitchen with her wine glass*) You were wonderful, Ben. Really wonderful.

Ben (*grins, extends his hand to Arthur as Leslie exits*) No hard feelings, okay?

Arthur (*shaking Ben's hand*) No hard feelings, guy. You're good. No. Better than good. Great. How's that?

Ben I don't know if I'm great . . . Not any more . . .

Arthur Come on, Ben, All City. All State. I can understand why the Steelers wanted to sign you up. You must have left skid marks all over Pittsburgh.

Ben I did.

Arthur I mean, guys hanging on to you, ten, fifteen yards, digging in your cleats, heading for the end zone.

Ben That's the way it was. Really.

Arthur (*puts an arm around Ben, squeezes his shoulder*) Hey, I believe it.

Ben This one kid, Washington Williams, he must have hung on to me for forty yards.

Arthur No shit. Forty yards? That's really something, Ben. (*Moves away.*) What about another beer?

Ben No, that's okay. (*Holds up his bottle.*) I've still got some left.

Arthur sets his wallet down, opens two beers, and then moves back to Ben. He takes Ben's beer bottle, sets it down, and then hands him the new beer.

Arthur (*opening the beers*) Come on, Ben. You won. What do you want to do? Just sit around? It's time to celebrate, guy.

Ben (*glances at his beer bottle, grins, shrugs*) Sure. Why not? I scored twelve, didn't I?

Arthur Twelve to six, buddy. (*Hands Ben the new beer.*) All the right moves.

Ben (*sipping his new beer, wandering*) I just kept my head, that's all. Remembered what it used to be like when we got down to the three-yard line. Coach used to call me over – tell me it was time to fly. 'Put on your goddamn wings, Cook.' That's what he used to say. (*Stops wandering, faces Arthur.*) It feels good, Arthur. It feels fantastic. Just to know I could still do it. That means a lot to me. Especially now. I mean, after the Rosemont and everything.

Arthur (*moves to Ben, puts an arm around Ben's shoulder*) I'm glad you're feeling good Ben. Real glad. Hell, you should feel good. You've been beating me all night. (*Moves back to his wallet, taking money out of it.*) Here you go. Forty bucks. Winner take all.

Ben Keep it, Arthur. Really. Money wasn't the point.

Arthur No? Then what was the point, Ben?

Ben (*shrugs*) Just winning.

Leslie re-enters the living room carrying a glass of wine and eating a piece of cheese on a cracker.

Arthur (*as Leslie re-enters*) Wrong, Ben. Money's always the point. Nobody plays for free any more. Not even us.

(*Holds out the money.*) You and your wife, you go out to dinner. Get yourselves a nice bottle of wine. (*Holds out the money.*) Here's fifty. Ten for the magic trick.

Ben Come on, Arthur. Put it away. Don't embarrass me.

Arthur suddenly jams the money into Ben's shirt pocket.

Arthur (*speaking with an edge*) Take the money.

Arthur moves away from Ben, tossing his wallet on top of his suit jacket, and then takes a long swig of beer. Leslie glances between Ben and Arthur, sensing the tension.

Ben (*takes the money out of his shirt pocket, holds it up to Arthur*) I won it fair and square, Arthur.

Leslie Of course you did, Ben.

Arthur (*smiles*) Hey, you won it fair and square, guy. Nothing to worry about. But see, the difference is, Ben, in Detroit, you earned your yardage. You went through guys, or you went around them. If you – (*indicates Leslie*) – hid behind cheerleaders, then you got 'Chickenshit' sprayed all over your locker.

Leslie (*laughs*) Arthur, it was a trick play, for God's sake. You fell for it, that's all.

Arthur Well, as I remember, trick plays didn't win championships in Detroit. Talent did it. Guts did it.

Ben (*slowing*) What are you saying? That I didn't have the talent? That I didn't have the guts? I just took you down, mister, and you ended up – (*Points at the floor.*) – eating wood. That ought to say something.

Arthur I missed a tackle in a living room. Big deal, right? Happens all the time, you have a few drinks. What do you think? You think it's going to get your name in the paper again?

Leslie Come on, Arthur. You wanted to win just as much as Ben did.

Ben I beat you, fella. That's good enough for me. I earned the yardage, pal. Every inch of it. Just like I earned the Rosemont last Tuesday night.

Arthur Right. The Rosemont. Let's talk about the Rosemont. I've got news for you, Ben. It was just another fire in Detroit City. We get them all day long here. What's the average? You ought to know. Every ten minutes, right? It's fire city, Ben. Page forty-two. That's how important it was.

Leslie It was important to Ben. That's all that counts.

Ben (*anger building*) I've got news for you, too, fella. It wasn't just another fire. Not to me. I could have died in it. A lot of people could have died in it. Human beings. You were sitting out here – what? Listening to your new speakers? And I was going up three flights to drag a woman out. You tell me – who had the better night? You or me? Who's got the memory, pal?

Arthur No, see, the way I look at it, Ben, the way most people would look at it, I mean, listening to you tell it, seems to me, you used a woman. That's all you did. She was just a ticket, wasn't she?

Ben I saw her hanging out of the window! You didn't see her. I saw the look on her face. You didn't see that either. That's what made me do it.

Leslie You don't have to defend yourself, Ben.

Ben (*to Leslie*) I mean, she was terrified. I've never seen terror like that.

Arthur But what'd it get you, Ben? I mean, outside of a paragraph in last week's *Free Press*.

Leslie He did save a woman! At least give him that!

Arthur You want to go home with him? Or maybe it's just Gil Henschel you want to fuck!

Leslie (*becoming frightened*) What's wrong with you?

Arthur You're out of a job, Benny. That's what really got you. What do you plan to do? Sell the rights to your story?

Ben I'm going to get my job back . . . I'm going to make them listen to me . . .

Arthur Well, if that's the plan, Benny, then I've got another flash for you.

Leslie Goddamn it, Arthur, he is a hero! He'll get his job back.

Arthur Yeah? Nobody but nobody cares about the Rosemont in this town. It's just another burned-out building in Detroit, Benny, and when they get enough money for the matches, they're just going to burn down ten more.

Ben Four hundred people lived in that hotel, and only one person died in it. That's firemen doing their job, fella . . . And nobody did it better than I did. I didn't just stand there. I did something about it. I did something brave. And that makes me a hero.

Arthur That's great, Ben, but what about the mortgage?

Ben It'll work out . . .

Leslie (*to Ben*) It will.

Arthur This is Detroit, Michigan, Benny. Nothing works out.

Leslie (*moving towards Ben*) Ben, just get out of here. Do it now.

Ben You listen to this, Arthur . . . When I brought her out, they hugged me. People I didn't even know. They had their arms around me. They wanted to give me money. Money. That's how important I was.

Arthur It was last week, Benny. Who even remembers?

Leslie Goddamn it, Arthur, you couldn't have done it! You wouldn't have even tried!

Arthur He gets paid to do it! Anybody could live your life, Benny! It wouldn't take a lot of imagination!

Ben (*struggling*) My life – my life is important . . .

Leslie (*moving towards it*) I'm getting his jacket!

Ben (*overlapping, trying to reach Arthur*) It's important! I've made it important . . . Isn't that what they teach us? Isn't that what you're supposed to do in this country? Nobody does it for you, you've got to do it yourself. I've been living in smoke for twenty-one years. That's got to mean something, doesn't it?

Arthur You chose the job, Benny! Not me!

Leslie (*holding up Ben's suit jacket*) Ben, it's time to go!

Arthur Go home, Benny! We've got to clean up the house.

Ben (*to Leslie*) I've coughed up ashes and soot so many times I've got a permanent rip in my throat . . . The 'Riots', I went without sleep for five days . . . I earned the Rosemont . . . I did . . .

Leslie Come on, Ben. It's time to go home. You're exhausted.

Ben (*ignoring Leslie, to Arthur*) I pulled out a woman . . . I got her down to the street . . .

Arthur (*faces Ben, his voice hard*) No, Benny, you pulled out a black woman! Big fucking mistake in this town! We could have been short one welfare cheque!

Ben, suddenly agonised, hurls his beer bottle behind him. It strikes the upstage wall and shatters; glass falls on the floor, beer runs down the wall.

Ben IT WAS A LIFE!

Leslie My God!

Arthur YOU FUCK!

Ben (*points a finger at Arthur*) They were going to let her burn up! I made sure it didn't happen!

Ben hugs himself and bends over, almost in pain, taking deep breaths. Arthur slowly sets his beer bottle down. Leslie, shocked, frightened, puts Ben's suit jacket down, and then slowly moves to the upstage wall, inspecting the damage.

(*shaking his head*) The *Free Press* was there . . . Jerry Giordano . . . And the only guy he interviewed was me! (*Hugs himself harder.*) That's got to mean something, doesn't it? That's got to be important, doesn't it? Everybody I know, they never got their names in the *Free Press*!

Arthur moves towards Ben.

Arthur What do you think, Benny? You think maybe it's time to clean it up?

Ben (*sotto, agitated, overlapping*) I saw her . . . She was up there . . . Third-floor window . . .

Leslie (*picking up a piece of glass*) My God!

Arthur (*glances at Leslie*) Don't touch it!

Ben They were just standing there . . .

Leslie It's soaking into the wood!

Arthur I said don't touch it!

Ben They didn't want to go in . . . They weren't going to get her . . .

Leslie I'll clean it up! Just let him go!

Ben There's a woman up there! You just gonna leave her?!

Arthur No, he's going to clean it up!

Ben You just gonna let her burn?!

Arthur This time he's going to clean it up!

Ben You just gonna let her die?!

Leslie You got him to throw the bottle! Isn't that enough?!

Arthur (*without looking at her*) He's going to clean it up!

Leslie If he cleans it up, it'll look even worse!

Arthur Doesn't matter!

Ben drops his arms to his sides and straightens up. He turns away from Arthur, spots his suit jacket, and begins to move towards it, almost shuffling.

Ben (*without looking*) I wasn't lying . . . I almost made the Steelers . . . I would have made the Steelers . . . There was a scout sitting in the McKeesport end zone . . . (*picking up his suit jacket*) Like he was waiting for me to come to him . . .

Arthur (*moving to Ben*) No, Ben, you're not leaving, not before you wipe up your little accident!

Ben (*pause*) What? Wipe up what?

Arthur What?! (*Turns Ben upstage, points.*) Take a goddamn look!

Leslie (*moving towards them*) Arthur, I don't want you fighting him!

Arthur He cleans it up, or he crawls out of here!

Ben (*running a hand through his hair*) I didn't do that, did I? I didn't spill it . . .

Arthur It didn't pop out of your hand!

Leslie (*takes Ben's arm and starts to lead him towards the front door*) Come on, Ben. Don't worry about the bottle.

Arthur pushes Leslie away from Ben.

Arthur He cleans it up!

Leslie Arthur, I swear, you touch him . . .

Arthur (*grabbing her wrist hard*) And what?! (*Raises her wrist higher.*) What?!

Ben I won't . . . I won't clean it up . . .

Arthur (*moving closer to Ben*) You clean it up, or guess what, Ben?! I'm going to rub your fucking nose in it!

Leslie You're not!

Arthur You watch me!

Leslie Stop it!

Arthur Why?! Because I care about what I own?!

Leslie It doesn't have a thing to do with what you own!

Arthur Nobody walks into this house and throws a bottle! Nobody! (*gesturing around the house*) All I've ever done is work for this! And if this isn't it, then you tell me, what is?! What?!

Ben (*beginning to put on his suit jacket, speaking calmly*) You're not going to make me do that, Arthur. No. Not after what I've done. I'm a hero. That's what I am.

Arthur (*pushes Ben backward towards the upstage wall*) Clean it up!

Leslie (*grabbing Arthur's arms with both hands*) No! Let him go!

Arthur whips his arms away from Leslie and pushes her away – hard. She stumbles and falls. Ben is still trying to put on his suit jacket, moving away from Arthur towards the front door.

Arthur (*grabs Ben from behind*) I said clean it up!

Leslie screams as Arthur throws Ben to the floor very hard.

NOW!

Ben hits the floor hard. He cries out. It is a cry of anguish. He huddles on the floor, struggling to get free of his suit jacket, and then covering his head with his arms.

Ben Go ahead! Hit me! Go on! Try it! Hit me! Hit me! I can take it! I'll . . . I'll show you! I can take anything! I've proved it! I ran around giants! Giants! Why don't you hit me?! What the hell is this stuff doing on the lawn? I didn't give the order to bring it down here! Take it back up! All of it! And glue those goddamn trophies back together!

Arthur, shocked, begins moving away from Ben. Leslie starts to move towards Ben, intending to help him, but then stops.

(*crawling on the floor*) I'm not afraid of you! I'm not afraid of anything! I ran up three flights! You're supposed to get a heart attack! I didn't get one! (*Stumbles to his feet. He moans. There is a dazed, wild expression on his face.*)

Leslie Ben? Arthur? Arthur, help him . . .

Arthur, almost frozen, frightened, looks at Ben and then away.

Ben (*rises, stumbling, staring upward*) Fight that fire, men! Goddamn it, lift those hoses higher! (*Spots Arthur, stumbles to him.*) What the hell are you standing around for?! (*Grabs him.*) You're a fireman, aren't you?! (*Shakes him.*) I don't give a good goddamn if she's black! We've got a job to do! The city of Detroit pays us to do our job! Not just when the colour's right! All the time! Now let's get in there! Well, fuck you then! I'm going in!

Ben pushes Arthur hard. Unresisting, Arthur stumbles backwards. Ben turns away from Arthur. Leslie starts to move towards Ben.

Ben, terrified, glances at the coffee table, and then stumbles to it, frantic, crawling under it, drawing his knees up to his chest, huddling, moaning.

Don't touch the pipes! Don't touch them! Watch the wires! Watch them! Hug the wall! Left foot on the wall! Keep it there! Where are you? Goddamn it, I know you're in here! The corners, man! Try the corners! Under the bed! Feel for legs! Feel for arms! Gotta save her . . . Gotta save her . . . A save like this doesn't come around twice! You don't have twenty-one more years! You bring her out, the bedroom goes back in the house, kiddo! This isn't just a fire! This is THE fire!

Ben stands up, unaware of the coffee table on his back. The coffee table and everything on it slides off him and crashes to the floor.

(*frantically, as he stands up*) Try the closet! She's got to be in the closet!

Ben looks around wildly, taking deep breaths, suddenly focusing on Leslie, his face exploding with joy, extending his arms towards her.

I'VE GOT HER! (*stumbling towards her*) I'VE GOT HER!

Leslie, terrified, starts to back away from Ben. He reaches out and grabs her wrist. She screams. He starts to pull her towards him.

(*as he pulls her, calming her*) It's all right. It's okay. I'm here now. Nothing's going to happen. You're safe. All we've got to do is get down to the street. They're waiting for us.

Leslie struggles against his grip and screams again.

(*trying to calm her*) But I'm here. You don't have to scream any more.

Arthur stumbles towards Ben and Leslie, slipping on the debris from the coffee table and falling to the floor. Ben pulls at Leslie harder, irritated by her resistance.

God Almighty, it's coming down! We've got to get out of here! It's going to flash over! I can feel it! You want to get out, don't you?!

Arthur (*stumbles to his feet and starts towards Ben and Leslie again*) Ben!

Ben turns towards Arthur and roars at him in anger.

Ben This is my save, fella! Back out!

Arthur stops, almost paralysed. Leslie yanks her arm away from Ben and starts to turn away. Ben grabs her, and tries to lift her up.

Leslie flails at him, breaking away from his right hand. Ben roars in anger and raises his right fist above his head, holding Leslie's arm with his left hand. Leslie, struggling to get away, looks up, sees Ben's fist aimed at her, screams, and then falls to her knees, trying to pull away from him.

Arthur (*crying out*) Ben, DON'T!

Ben's fist begins to shake.

(*crying out again, pleading*) DON'T!

Ben's whole body begins to tremble. He turns towards Arthur, still holding on to Leslie's wrist.

Ben What do you mean she's dead?! Work on her! Bring her back, for God's sake! (*Turns back to Leslie.*) You're not dead! You're alive! I saved you! Didn't you think I'd save you?

Leslie pulls her hand away from Ben. Ben gently embraces her. Leslie, frozen, doesn't embrace him.

I saved you . . . I saved you . . .

Leslie gently embraces Ben.

You didn't have to die . . . I saved you . . . I saved you . . . I . . . I . . . I . . .

Ben holds Leslie in an embrace. Leslie holds Ben in an embrace. Pause. Leslie slowly pulls away from Ben. He lets her go. She backs away from him. Ben looks around suddenly, groans, and buries his face in his hands. Arthur turns away from him. Leslie stands up, wraps her arms around herself and takes deep breaths. Pause. Leslie takes a few hesitant steps towards Ben, and then stops. Pause.

Leslie (*hardly audible*) Ben? (*Pause. Louder*) Ben?

Ben doesn't respond. Leslie looks at Arthur. Arthur, frozen, stares at the floor. Leslie moves to Ben's suit jacket. She picks it up and moves to Ben, holding out the jacket.

Ben?

Ben doesn't respond. Leslie gently helps him up.

(*holding out the suit jacket*) Ben?

Ben slowly takes his suit jacket. It makes no sense to him. He holds it upside down. The flask falls to the floor. Leslie takes the coat back from him, goes behind him, and helps him on with his suit jacket. She picks up the flask and holds it out to him. He takes it. He stares at it, and then looks up.

Ben (*softly, staring straight ahead*) I didn't mean to barge in . . . I have to go home now . . . It's late . . . My Gloria's probably all worried . . . I have to talk to her . . .

Leslie moves to the closet, opens it, takes out Ben's raincoat, and then moves back to him with it.

Leslie (*holding out the coat*) Here . . . Here's your coat, Ben.

Ben takes his coat and hugs it against himself. Time passes. Ben slowly moves to the front door.

Ben?

Ben stops. He doesn't turn around. Arthur doesn't look at Ben or Leslie. Leslie moves towards Ben and stops.

I loved watching the firetrucks . . . When I was a little girl . . . I really did. I'd wait on the corner, and when the truck came by, I'd . . . I'd stand on my toes, and I'd wave up to all the firemen. And they'd wave back. Lean down and smile . . . It always made me feel secure. That's what it made me feel . . .

Time passes. Ben moves to the front door, opens it, and exits the house, leaving the door open. Leslie moves to the door, turns on the porch light, and stares out of the door after Ben, watching him walk home. Time passes. Arthur slowly turns towards the coffee-table debris, moves to it, bends down, and picks up a cigarette. He bends down again and picks up the table lighter. He lights the cigarette, and then moves to the couch, sitting down. He smokes and stares straight ahead. Time passes. Leslie closes the front door and turns off the porch light. She moves slowly towards the couch, stepping on broken glass. She stops at the end of the couch and stares at Arthur. She slowly moves to him and sits down next to him. They do not look at each other. Arthur continues to smoke. Time passes. She starts to reach over to touch him, her hand pausing in mid-air. She slowly places her hand on his arm, keeping it there. They do not look at each other. The lights very slowly fade to darkness.

Blackout.